LEARNING
ICT
with
ENGLISH

Other titles in the Teaching ICT through the Primary Curriculum series:

Learning ICT in the Arts
Andrew Hamill
1-84312-313-4

Learning ICT in the Humanities
Tony Pickford
1-84312-312-6

Learning ICT with Maths
Richard Bennett
1-84312-310-X

Learning ICT with Science
Andrew Hamill
1-84312-311-8

Progression in Primary ICT
Richard Bennett, Andrew Hamill and Tony Pickford
1-84312-308-8

LEARNING ICT with ENGLISH

Richard Bennett

David Fulton Publishers

David Fulton Publishers Ltd
The Chiswick Centre, 414 Chiswick High Road, London W4 5TF

www.fultonpublishers.co.uk
www.onestopeducation.co.uk

First published in Great Britain in 2006 by David Fulton Publishers

10 9 8 7 6 5 4 3 2 1

David Fulton Publishers is a division of Granada Learning Limited

British Library Cataloguing in Publication Data
A catalogue record for this book is available from the British Library.

ISBN: 1-84312-309-6 (EAN: 978184312 3095)

Typeset by Servis Filmsetting Ltd, Manchester
Printed and bound in Great Britain

Contents

CD contents

Resources and links (MS Word)
Certificate Read-Me (Text file)

Project 1

- Project 1 Completion Certificate (MS Word)
- Project 1 Completion 'Star' Certificate (MS Word)
- *Little Red Engine* by Mike Matson: downloaded from the *MAPE Big Books* website – http://www.mape.org.uk/activities/bigbooks/index.htm
- *Where do Hedgehogs Go?* by Celia Burley: downloaded from the *MAPE Big Books* website – http://www.mape.org.uk/activities/bigbooks/index.htm
- *Information Around Us: Sounds*: downloaded from the *MAPE Big Books* website – http://www.mape.org.uk/activities/bigbooks/index.htm
- *Muddy Time* by Heather Govier: downloaded from the *MAPE Big Books* website – http://www.mape.org.uk/activities/bigbooks/index.htm
- *Big Book Maker* by Mike Matson: downloaded from the *MAPE* website – http://www.mape.org.uk/activities/index.htm
- Instructions for using the Big Book Maker (MS Word)
- Project 1 Evaluation (MS Word)

Project 2

- Project 2 Completion Certificate (MS Word)
- Project 2 Completion 'Star' Certificate (MS Word)
- Example talking stories created using *2Create A Story* (2Simple): reproduced with permission from Julie Steer at 2Simple
    - *Birthday Cake*
    - *Michael Ladybird*
    - *Chelsea Spider*
    - *Spaceship*
- Word bank for *Gilly the Hen* (Textease)
- Word bank of prepositions (Text file for use in any word processor)
- Project 2 Evaluation (MS Word)

Project 3

- Project 3 Completion Certificate (MS Word)
- Project 3 Completion 'Star' Certificate (MS Word)
- A flow chart showing the structure of this example story (MS Word/JPEG image)
- Examples of branching stories
  - *Little Story* – a three-page example of a branching story using *Textease*
  - *Deathtrap Dare* – *Textease* branching story written by Year 5 children
  - *Dilemma* – a moral dilemma branching story similar to *Kate's Choice* (MS Word)
  - *King Midas* – the story of King Midas told by different narrators (*Flash* presentation produced with *2Create* (2Simple). Reproduced with permission from Julie Steer at 2Simple
- Template booklets for *Textease* branching stories
  - A4 booklet with two choices per page
  - A4 booklet with two choices per page (colour version)
  - Screen-sized booklet with two choices per page
- Project 3 Evaluation (MS Word)

Project 4

- Project 4 Completion Certificate (MS Word)
- Project 4 Completion 'Star' Certificate (MS Word)
- A series of video tutorials for using **Sound Recorder**:
  - Starting **Sound Recorder**
  - Setting the volume
  - Recording sounds
  - Inserting a sound
  - Combining sound files
  - Deleting part of a sound
- Project 4 Evaluation (MS Word)

Project 5

- Project 5 Completion Certificate (MS Word)
- Project 5 Completion 'Star' Certificate (MS Word)
- Real crime stories from local newspapers (MS Word)
- An example newspaper story of a crime (MS Word)
- A record card for the villain in the crime story (Text file)
- A Wanted poster for the above villain (MS Word)
- A database file of villains
  - Tab delimited text file (tsv)
  - Comma separated text file (csv)
  - *Textease Database* file
- Face picture elements for drawing programs
- Project 5 Evaluation (MS Word)

Project 6
- Project 6 Completion Certificate (MS Word)
- Project 6 Completion 'Star' Certificate (MS Word)
- Skeleton and full stories (Text files)
- Project 6 Evaluation (MS Word)

Project 7
- Project 7 Completion Certificate (MS Word)
- Project 7 Completion 'Star' Certificate (MS Word)
- Template for the children's storyboards (MS Word)
- Example storyboard (JPEG image)
- Storyboard template (MS Word)
- Project 7 Evaluation (MS Word)

Project 8
- Project 8 Completion Certificate (MS Word)
- Project 8 Completion 'Star' Certificate (MS Word)
- Example score card (MS Word)
- Template document for scripting or storyboarding (MS Word)
- Project 8 Evaluation (MS Word)

Project 9
- Project 9 Completion Certificate (MS Word)
- Project 9 Completion 'Star' Certificate (MS Word)
- Project 9 Evaluation (MS Word)
- *Web browsing with Internet Explorer and Managing Favourites* booklet (MS Word)

Project 10
- Project 10 Completion Certificate (MS Word)
- Project 10 Completion 'Star' Certificate (MS Word)
- A *Macbeth* webquest (example)
  - a website
  - a zipped folder containing the website for transfer to the children's computers
- Storyboard template (MS Word)
- Example storyboard (pdf file, reproduced with permission from the Teachit website)
- Project 10 Evaluation (MS Word)

Acknowledgements

The author and publishers would like to thank the following for permission to reproduce materials in this book and on the accompanying CD:

Mike Matson of MAPE, for the Teacher's Notes for Big Book Maker (see Project 1 on the CD).

Roger Reeling of MAPE for copies of the Big Books included on the CD.

Julie Steer of 2Simple Software for examples of work produced using 2Create a Story and 2Create.

Helen Collins of Whitefriars First and Middle School (Wealdstone) for examples of children's work reproduced on the CD.

Introduction

This book is based on the belief that the integration of information and communication technology (ICT) and subject teaching is of benefit to children's development through the Foundation Stage, Key Stage 1 and Key Stage 2. It focuses on ICT in the context of English and literacy. By incorporating some of the powerful ICT tools described in this book in your planning for English, the quality of your teaching and children's learning will improve. Similarly, by contextualising the children's ICT experience in meaningful literacy projects, children's ICT capability will be enhanced and extended. *Learning ICT with English* is one of a series of ICT books: Teaching ICT through the Primary Curriculum. The core book for the series, *Progression in Primary ICT*, provides a more detailed discussion of the philosophy behind the approach and offers an overview and a planning matrix for all the projects described in the series.

The activities that are presented here offer practical guidance and suggestions for both teachers and trainees. For experienced teachers and practitioners there are ideas for ways that ICT can be developed through the areas of learning and literacy and the primary English curriculum using ICT tools with which you are familiar. For less confident or less experienced users of ICT there are recommendations for resources and step-by-step guides aimed at developing your confidence and competence with ICT as you prepare the activities for your children.

The activities are related to the Foundation Stage areas of learning, the National Curriculum Programmes of Study (PoS) and the national framework for literacy. In some activities, such as Project 5: *Villains* and Project 9: *Creating an information website*, the emphasis is on finding things out with ICT. Other projects, e.g. Project 3: *Branching stories* and Project 10: *A* Macbeth *webquest*, offer opportunities for developing ideas and making things happen using ICT tools. Children are provided with purposeful opportunities to exchange and share information in most of the projects but a particular emphasis is placed on this in Project 2: *Making talking books* and Project 6: *Imaginative e-mail.* Throughout all the projects, ways in which children can reflect on their use of ICT or explore its use in society are identified. Although the projects are clearly located in literary contexts, many could be easily adapted to other subjects.

The projects do not provide an exhaustive or definitive list of ICT opportunities in English teaching. Instead, they are tried and tested sequences of activities, adaptable across the age-range, which ensure that high quality learning in ICT is accompanied by high quality learning in a literacy-related context. The projects are closely linked to relevant units in the Qualifications and Curriculum Authority (QCA) schemes of work for ICT and guidance is provided on how they could be used to supplement, augment, extend or replace many of these units. Although the projects are not future-proof, they have been designed to take advantage of some of the latest technologies now available in primary schools, such as interactive whiteboards, internet-linked computers and digital cameras.

A note on resources

Investment has improved the level of resources for the teaching of ICT in primary schools in recent years. The arrangement and availability of resources, however, still varies greatly from school to school. Some schools have invested heavily in centralised resources, setting up networked computer rooms or ICT suites. Others have gone down the route of networking the whole school, using wired or wireless technologies, with desktop or laptop computers being available in every classroom. Some schools have combined the two approaches, so that children have access to a networked suite and classroom computers. This book does not attempt to prescribe or promote a particular type of arrangement of computer hardware, but does make some assumptions in relation to the management of those resources. These assumptions are:

- The teacher has access to a large computer display for software demonstration and the sharing of children's work – this could be in the form of an interactive whiteboard (IWB), a data projector and large screen or a large computer monitor.

- Pupils (in groups or as individuals) have access to computers for hands-on activities – this may be in an ICT suite or by using a smaller number of classroom computers, perhaps on a rota basis.

- The school has internet access, and at least one networked computer is linked to a large display, as described above.

- Pupils have access to internet-linked computers and the school has a policy for safe use of the internet.

- Teachers and pupils have access to a range of software packages, including a web browser, 'office' software (such as a word processor) and some 'educational' software. Although this book makes some recommendations with regard to appropriate software, it also suggests alternatives that could be used, if a specific package is not available.

The projects

Each project is presented using the following format:

⊙ a Fact Card which gives a brief overview of the project content and how it links to curriculum requirements and documentation;

⊙ detailed guidance on how to teach a sequence of ICT activities in a subject context;

⊙ information on pupils' prior learning required by the project;

⊙ guidance for the teacher on the skills, knowledge and understandings required to teach the project, including step-by-step guidance on specific tasks, skills and tools;

⊙ clear and specific information about what the children will learn in ICT and the subject;

⊙ guidance on how to adapt the project for older or more experienced pupils;

⊙ guidance on how to modify the project for younger or less experienced pupils;

⊙ a summary of reasons to teach the project, including reference to relevant curriculum documentation and research.

National Curriculum coverage

The ICT activities described in this book are those which are most relevant to English learning and hence not all areas of the ICT curriculum have been covered. The core text for the series, *Progression in Primary ICT*, shows how coverage of the ICT curriculum can be achieved by selecting the most appropriate subject-related activities for your teaching situation and how progression in ICT capability can be accomplished through meaningful contexts. Figure 1 provides an indication of the aspects of ICT which are addressed by the projects in this book.

Focus age groups for each project

Figure 2 provides an indication of the age group for which each project has been written. However, most activities can be adapted for older or younger children and guidance on how this can be done is provided in the information for each project.

Coverage of ICT National Curriculum Programmes of Study by each project

Key Stage 1

Projects:	1	2	3	4	5	6	7	8	9	10
Finding things out										
1a. gather information from a variety of sources	✓									
1b. enter and store information in a variety of forms		✓								
1c. retrieve information that has been stored		✓								
Developing ideas and making things happen										
2a. use text, tables, images and sound to develop their ideas	✓	✓								
2b. select from and add to information they have retrieved for particular purposes										
2c. plan and give instructions to make things happen										
2d. try things out and explore what happens in real and imaginary situations										
Exchanging and sharing information										
3a. share their ideas by presenting information in a variety of forms		✓								
3b. present their completed work effectively		✓								

Key Stage 2

Projects:	1	2	3	4	5	6	7	8	9	10
Finding things out										
1a. talk about what information they need and how they can find and use it					✓	✓			✓	✓
1b. prepare information for development using ICT, including selecting suitable sources, finding information, classifying it and checking it for accuracy					✓				✓	✓
1c. interpret information, to check it is relevant and reasonable and to think about what might happen if there were any errors or omissions					✓	✓			✓	✓
Developing ideas and making things happen										
2a. develop and refine ideas by bringing together, organising and reorganising text, tables, images and sound as appropriate			✓	✓	✓		✓	✓	✓	✓
2b. create, test, improve and refine sequences of instructions to make things happen and to monitor events and respond to them								✓	✓	
2c. use simulations and explore models in order to answer 'What if . . .?' questions, to investigate and evaluate the effect of changing values and to identify patterns and relationships										
Exchanging and sharing information										
3a. share and exchange information in a variety of forms, including e-mail				✓	✓	✓	✓	✓	✓	✓
3b. be sensitive to the needs of the audience and think carefully about the content and quality when communicating information			✓	✓	✓	✓	✓	✓	✓	✓

Figure 1

Year groups covered by each project

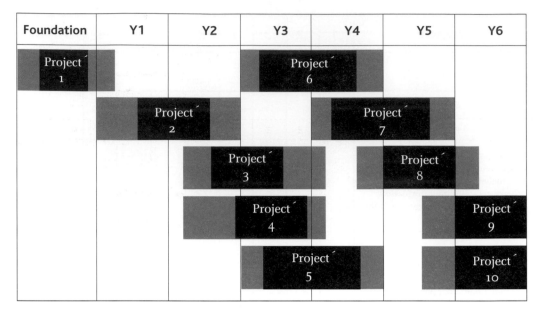

Figure 2

Links to the QCA scheme of work for ICT

Figure 3 indicates the relationship between the projects included in this book and the QCA ICT units in Key Stages 1 and 2. The key indicates which QCA units can be replaced, supported or extended by the projects in this book.

Links to the QCA scheme of work for ICT in Key Stages 1 and 2

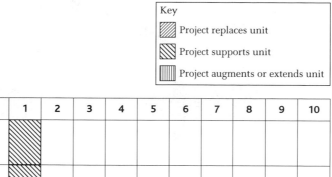

Key
▨	Project replaces unit
▧	Project supports unit
▥	Project augments or extends unit

Projects:	1	2	3	4	5	6	7	8	9	10
Unit 1A: An introduction to modelling	▨									
Unit 1C: The information around us	▨									
Unit 2A: Writing stories: communicating information using text		▨								
Unit 2B: Creating pictures		▨								
Unit 2E: Questions and answers					▥					
Unit 3A: Combining text and graphics		▨	▨		▨					
Unit 3B: Manipulating sound				▨						
Unit 3C: Introduction to databases					▨					
Unit 3E: E-mail						▧				
Unit 4A: Writing for different audiences			▨	▨	▥		▥			
Unit 5B: Analysing data and asking questions: using complex searches					▥					
Unit 5C: Evaluating information, checking accuracy and questioning plausibility									▧	▧
Unit 6A: Multimedia presentation			▥				▥	▧	▨	
Unit 6D: Using the internet to search large databases and to interpret information									▨	▨

Figure 3

Project Fact Card: Project 1: Using talking books

Who is it for?

- 4- to 5-year-olds (NC Levels 0–1)

What will the children do?

- Explore and describe the structure of an interactive talking book/story

What should the children know already?

- How books work
- That the mouse can be used to control the pointer on screen
- How to select or activate objects or buttons on screen with the mouse button

What do I need to know?

- How to load and run CD-ROM-based programs
- How to demonstrate the use of the mouse
- The basic structure and content of the talking books or stories used
- The technical features of the talking story/ies to be emphasised
- How to adjust the sound volume
- How to attach headphones or a listening unit to the computer (if required)

What resources will I need?

- A Big Book
- An electronic version of the same Big Book
- A large screen (e.g. projector, interactive whiteboard or large monitor)

What will the children learn?

- How to interact with text, images and animations through use of the mouse
- That computers can store and present information as text, pictures, sounds and moving images
- To associate text with words and sounds (phonological awareness)

How to challenge the more able

- Select talking stories which require more interaction with text than images
- Use support staff to work alongside the children to ask challenging questions or to seek suggestions about the structure and content of the story

How to support the less able

- Select stories which require minimal interaction or which have simple repetitive forms of interaction on each page
- Use support staff to work alongside the children

Why teach this?

- It addresses ICT NC KS1 PoS statements 1a, 2a
- It supports and augments QCA ICT Scheme of Work Units 1A, 1C
- It builds on English NC KS1 PoS statements En1, 2a, 2b, 9c; En2, 3a–c, 6g (6a–f)
- It addresses NLS units for Reception Terms 1, 3, 6, 8, 9
- Research indicates that talking stories can enhance interest and motivation in reluctant readers, particularly boys, if used in conjunction with conventional reading materials

Using talking books

What will the children do?

Activity 1: Comparing an electronic book with a real book

Read a conventional book (or part) to the children in the conventional way. Emphasise the format and structure of the book together with salient features of the way the text works.

Present the same story (or part) in electronic form. After introducing the electronic book, ask the children to suggest ways in which the electronic version might work. For example, 'How do you think we should turn to the next page?'; 'What do you think will happen if I click on the beach ball?' If an interactive whiteboard is being used, the children could come out and 'test' their ideas.

Discuss the differences they have noticed between the paper-based version of the story and the electronic version.

Activity 2: Reading an electronic book in pairs

Match pairs of children for reading ability or ensure a confident reader is well briefed on how to work alongside one who is less confident. Depending on the availability of computers and electronic books, the children could explore the same story (in turn) or read stories matched to their interests or capabilities.

Ask the children to explore the story and remember a particular part or 'feature' of the story which they enjoy. The pairs provide feedback on their favourite parts in the plenary or sharing session.

Activity 3: Changing partners

Pair the children with a different partner who has read a different story. The 'expert' child takes the 'novice' through the story. The 'expert' could be instructed to ask the 'novice' to anticipate what happens next at key points in the story or to predict the animations and/or sounds.

Swap stories so the novice now becomes the expert.

As a group, discuss differences and similarities with the way electronic stories are presented. If stories from the same series are used, there may be several similarities in presentation approaches.

Activity 4: Applying their knowledge

Read a new paper-based story to the children and at intervals ask them to suggest ideas for an electronic version. Show them the electronic version and discuss the differences between their ideas and the electronic interpretation.

What should the children know already?

How books work

To appreciate the differences between conventional story books and electronic versions, children ought to be familiar with at the least the following features:

⊙ that books have a title and an author (and illustrator);

⊙ how stories are sequenced and structured;

⊙ that there is usually a link between the illustrations and the narrative.

That the mouse can be used to control the pointer on screen

Often referred to as 'mouse skills', electronic books are an ideal medium for reinforcing and extending children's knowledge and understanding of the relationship between the mouse and the on-screen pointer. Concepts and skills which can be reinforced include:

⊙ co-ordination of mouse movement and pointer motion;

⊙ that changes in pointer shape are dependent on the area of the screen being explored;

⊙ that they can right click and double click.

How to select or activate objects or buttons on screen with the mouse button

Because the use of the mouse is, to most users, automatic, it is all too easy to assume that some of the most fundamental concepts and skills associated with the use of the mouse do not need to be learnt or taught. Some of these basic skills can be reinforced through interacting with a talking book, but children's use of the computer should be monitored in the early stages to ensure they have sufficient competence with basic use of the mouse to be able to navigate through the book's features.

What resources will I need?

A Big Book

The book does not need to be a 'Big Book' provided it is sufficiently large for the children to see the illustrations and page layout from time to time during your reading.

An electronic version of the same Big Book

A range of electronic books (and talking stories) is available on the internet:

⊙ Sebastian Swan's Infant Explorer – www.sebastianswan.org.uk

⊙ Lancashire Grid for Learning (LGfL) big books online – www.lancsngfl.ac.uk

⊙ MAPE Big Books – www.mape.org.uk/activities

⊙ MAPE Big Book Maker – www.mape.org.uk/activities

Some of the Big Books from the MAPE website and the Big Book Maker are reproduced (with permission) on the CD-ROM which accompanies this book.

A large screen (e.g. projector, interactive whiteboard or large monitor)

It is not essential to have an interactive whiteboard for this project. A data projector or a large monitor screen will be sufficient provided all the children can see the screen comfortably.

What do I need to know?

How to load and run CD-ROM-based programs

In most cases, talking books are provided on CD-ROMs which run automatically (autorun) after being inserted into the CD drive. Occasionally, you might come across a computer which has not been set up to autorun CD-ROMs. If this is the case, after inserting the disc, click on the **Start** button in the bottom left corner of the screen and then click on **Run . . .** which should appear in the menu which pops up.

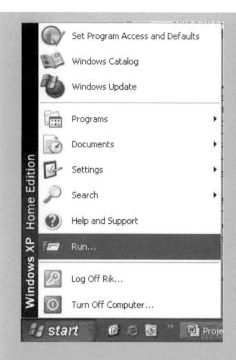

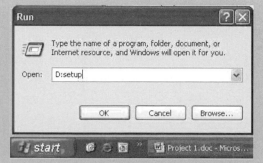

Try typing in **D:setup** and clicking the **OK** button. If this does not work, try changing the **D** to the letter **E** or **F**. Failing that type in **D:run** and click **OK**. If in doubt, consult the documentation which came with the CD-ROM.

How to demonstrate the use of the mouse

Computer mice vary in design and some are easier for young children to use than others. Many children find smaller mice, such as those for laptop computers, more suited to their hands. If you have access to a data projector or large monitor screen, a wireless mouse can prove useful for demonstrating basic skills as it can be passed around from child to child. Alternatives to the standard mouse, such as a tracker ball, touch-tablet or a touch sensitive screen (e.g. a tablet PC) can sometimes be helpful for children with co-ordination problems or restricted movement.

A tracker ball can be used in place of a mouse

The basic structure and content of the talking books or stories used

Preparation for any ICT-based activity is very important and no less so with talking books. In addition to knowing the story you should explore the additional features such as the animations and sound controls. Some talking stories are configurable, allowing the teacher to enable or disable some features such as sounding the words when clicked. In some talking books, the speed at which the text is read, the colour of highlighting, the type of voice and even the language (English, Spanish, Urdu, etc.) can be modified.

The technical features of the talking story/ies to be emphasised

The following ought to be mastered by you and/or your teaching assistants before using talking books with children. Unfortunately, there is no common pattern to the way in which different software companies present the following and so you may need to consult the manual accompanying the story.

- Where to find the title and author/illustrator (i.e. an electronic story is not written by machine)
- How to navigate through the story (e.g. forward and back through screen or 'pages')
- How or if words can be sounded or read
- How to access the teacher/adult controls, what they are and what they do

How to adjust the sound volume

Some talking stories include teacher controls to set the maximum volume level to prevent children from increasing the volume beyond a pre-set limit.

How to attach headphones or a listening unit to the computer (if required)

Just as a listening unit can be plugged into a tape recorder for shared listening, a listening unit can be connected to the audio output socket of most computers. The audio socket is often colour coded green and is located on the back panel of older computers or on the front of more recent machines. If the plug on the listening unit does not fit into the socket, an adaptor plug might be required. If uncertain, seek technical assistance to avoid the risk of damaging either the computer or the listening unit.

What will the children learn?

How to interact with text, images and animations through use of the mouse

Learning how to use a mouse successfully requires more knowledge and understanding than the development of mouse co-ordination skills. Making predictions about what might happen if something is clicked, and knowing that a double click or a right click might produce a different outcome, are significant foundation concepts. To develop independence, children need opportunities to explore, to predict, to try things out and to see the effect of their actions. This investigational/problem-solving approach is sometimes labelled 'discovery' or 'What if . . .?' learning. While computer-based activities such as this can never replace real-life experience, the advantage of a computer-based activity is that it can be constrained and controlled and that the outcomes are safe and predictable.

That computers can store and present information as text, pictures, sounds and moving images

Multimedia is a combination of text, images, animation, video sound and hyperlinks presented through a computer screen. A hyperlink is a piece of text or part of the screen (sometimes called a hot-spot or presented as a 'button' or icon) which, when clicked, makes something happen. For example, clicking on a word may cause it to be read aloud; clicking on an image may make it animate; clicking on an arrow icon may take the user to a different screen. The importance of exploring a computer screen by moving the mouse pointer around and clicking to see what might happen should not be underestimated as this lays the foundation for helping children develop the skills and knowledge they need to access, manipulate and ultimately present information in a range of forms and formats. Developing this 'multimedia literacy' is important for children in today's (and tomorrow's) world.

To associate text with words and sounds (phonological awareness)

The great virtue in being able to click on text and hear it being read, while simultaneously having each syllable or word highlighted on screen, is that it enhances phonological awareness more effectively than any other method. The sound and highlighting can be faultlessly synchronised, whereas a finger or pointer could fall behind or leap ahead. Some talking stories (and talking word processors) permit the child to click on individual words or parts of words and have them sounded out individually. This can be particularly effective for shared or guided reading activities – for example, finding all the occurrences of a particular phonic blend or keyword.

Challenging the more able and supporting the less able: modifying the project for older and younger pupils

Selecting talking stories appropriate for the needs of the children

Some talking stories place more emphasis on the animations than they do on the text. As a consequence, most children tend to ignore the text because the animations are more stimulating. In some stories, the animations can be turned off, or restricted. Alternatively, stories with fewer animated options can be selected for those who need the challenge of engaging more with the text.

Knowing the content and structure of talking books can help ensure that they are selected to address the needs of the children. In addition, accessing websites and online databases providing outlines and evaluations of educational software can extend your knowledge of what is available.

The TEEM (Teachers Evaluating Educational Multimedia) website (www.teem.org.uk) provides information and case studies about the content and relevance of educational software carried out by practising teachers in real classrooms.

The Becta Educational Software Database (BESD) (http://besd.becta.org.uk) also provides information about the educational content and effectiveness of a range of software.

Using support staff to work alongside the children to ask challenging questions or to seek suggestions about the structure and content of the story

One way to increase the level of challenge is have a teaching assistant or trained parent asking questions at opportune moments as the child works through a talking story. Alternatively, the adult can be there to guide and remediate as required. It should not be assumed that talking stories obviate the need for an adult to intervene while the children are working at the computer.

Why teach this?

QCA ICT Unit 1A: *An introduction to modelling* focuses on developing children's understanding that computers can simulate real-life or imaginary experiences, albeit in a simplified form. However, there are very few simulations and adventure programs which are suitable for young children. The most notable of the latter are *Elf Tales* (Sherston) and *Granny's Garden* (4mation). However, while these programs are well crafted, they can be quite time consuming to work through and require considerable preparation by the teacher to be successful. This project can be used to augment the unit or to replace the simulation and adventure game activities.

Unit 1C: *The information around us* specifically mentions the use of a talking book as a means of raising pupils' awareness of the different ways in which information can be presented. It would be useful therefore if, before working through the unit, the children were already familiar with talking stories and had discussed their structure and presentation. Alternatively, the project could be integrated with Unit 1C and the focus shifted more to computer-based information sources.

Providing an opportunity for children to interact with talking stories not only enhances their literacy skills; it also lays the foundation for skills and knowledge in accessing information presented electronically. Developing awareness that information on a computer screen, unlike a TV screen, can be responsive to the children's actions with the mouse pointer and that certain actions result in particular effects (e.g. clicking on a button) is very important for helping them interact with computer-based and web-based information sources. Working with talking stories also helps children appreciate that information and entertainment can be effectively presented in the form of text, images, animations, video clips and sound.

By working with talking books which present the children with information through multimedia, the children are learning how the same sort of information can be presented in different, but complementary, ways. Thus, when they come to start preparing their own talking stories and interactive information sources (see Projects 2, 3, 8 and 10) they will have had experience of different forms of multimedia presentation on which they can draw.

Lancy and Hayes (1988) found that young children spent considerably longer reading interactive books than they did conventional books. While the measure of time alone is not an indicator that learning is taking place, it stands to reason that the longer a child engages with text, the more opportunities there are for learning to take place. Jane Medwell has been studying the impact of talking books and word processors for many years and she concludes that talking books are particularly useful in helping to improve a child's accuracy in reading, especially if the talking book is one which is also being read by the teacher (Medwell 1995, 1998).

See also *Humanities* Project 1 (*Decision making with a mouse*) for related activities.

References and further reading

Lancy, D. and Hayes, B. (1988) 'Interactive fiction and the reluctant reader', *English Journal*, 77 (7): 42–6.

Medwell, J. (1995) 'Talking books for teaching reading', *Microscope*, (46), 22–5.

Medwell, J. (1998) 'The Talking Books Project: some further insights into the use of talking books to develop reading', *Reading*, 32 (1), April, 3–8.

Project Fact Card: Project 2: Making talking books

Who is it for?

- 6- to 7-year-olds (NC Levels 1–2)

What will the children do?

- Discuss the structure and content of talking stories they know then help to plan a talking story. Each pair will write and record one page (or more) of a talking story and then the whole class will evaluate the effectiveness of their talking story

What should the children know already?

- What a talking story is and how it is structured
- How to type simple text into a word processor or similar package

What do I need to know?

- How to structure a simple story with a repetitive theme
- How to enter text, images and sounds into the program
- (Optional) How to scan or import digital images into a computer and insert them into the program used for the story

What resources will I need?

- An example of a CD-ROM-based talking story
- A Big Book of a story with a repetitive theme
- A program suitable for making a talking story
- A computer which is less than four years old

What will the children learn?

- That computers can be used to manipulate text, images and sounds
- That computer-based talking stories are written by authors and not computers
- How to enter text, images and sounds into a computer
- How to evaluate a piece of work completed on a computer and suggest improvements

How to challenge the more able

- Give them more responsibility for recording and inserting the sounds and images
- Expect more demanding content for their pages
- Ask them to support those with less experience

How to support the less able

- Provide more support when they are working on the computer
- Structure the activity more, for example through the use of template documents, writing frames or word banks
- Pair the children so that a less experienced child is working with a more experienced child

Why teach this?

- It addresses ICT NC KS1 PoS statements 1b, 1c, 2a, 3a, 3b
- It complements QCA ICT Scheme of Work Units 2A, 2B, 3A
- It addresses English NC KS1 PoS statements En2, 3a–e; En3, 1a, 1c, 1f, 2b, 2c, 7a, 7c
- It complements NLS units for Year 2 Term 1 Text 9; Year 2 Term 2 Texts 13, 15
- It provides a context for shared and collaborative writing

Making talking books

The activities described here are aimed at Year 2 children, but the project could easily be carried out with any age group in Key Stages 1 and 2. See guidance on supporting the less able for adapting the activities for younger children and the guidance on challenging the more able for modifications for those who are older.

What will the children do?

Activity 1: Discussing the structure and content of talking stories the children know

This initial activity helps set the context for the activities which follow. By Year 2 the children should be familiar with CD-ROM-based talking stories of various types and should be able to recall their favourites. To refresh their memories it might be useful to demonstrate a talking story (or part of a talking story).

Focus your questioning on the differences between a talking story and a conventional text-based story. The similarities and differences should be noted, for example:

Similarities

⊙ The story is told through a series of pages

⊙ Text and images help to tell the story

⊙ The stories have an author and an illustrator

Differences

⊙ The book is easy to carry around

⊙ The text can be read out loud by the computer

⊙ Some of the pictures can be animated

Show the rest of the story and discuss how the plot could have developed as an alternative to that portrayed.

Tell the children they are going to become the authors of a talking story.

Activity 2: Planning a talking story

Remind the children about the similarities and differences between a talking story and a conventional story. Read a familiar story which has a repetitive theme, for example *Rosie's Walk* (Hutchins 2001), *Not Now, Bernard* (McKee 1996), *The Very Hungry Caterpillar* (Carle 2002).

Dissect the story with them, emphasising the way it is divided into pages – and how the pages are similar to each other and yet slightly different.

Ask the children to suggest their own story, or a variation on the story which they have just heard. Plot their ideas for each page on a chart. If the children are to work in pairs on the computer it is important that there are sufficient pages for each pair. Failing that, the story could be written or another story could be plotted.

Activity 3: Each pair writes their page of the story

If the story has been carefully selected, then the amount of typing which is required of each pair should be minimal. Depending on the software package being used, you might be able to prepare a template document together with a word bank which provides the children with the framework sentence(s) and key-words they will need. An example of a word bank of prepositions for this story is provided on the CD-ROM accompanying this book.

Activity 3a: The children illustrate their page from the story

Ask each pair to produce an illustration for their page. The children could work together or produce individual illustrations. The illustrations could be made using conventional materials such as crayons or paints, but the size of the picture will be restricted by the size of scanner to which you have access.

Alternatively, the children could produce an illustration using a computer-based painting program. By Year 1, they should have some familiarity with a painting program and ought to be able to produce something on the computer which is appropriate. However, children have difficulty controlling the mouse when using a painting program and can become frustrated that the picture they are trying to draw does not appear as they intended. In this case, you might consider providing them with Clip Art images which they can insert into their pictures.

A third alternative is for the children to take digital photos to illustrate the story. These can be images from locations around the school, in which case the story might need to reflect this at the planning stage, or could feature children dressing up to re-enact the story. In this case the pictures could arise from a drama lesson.

Finally, the children could take digital photos of cuddly toys or puppets acting out the story. Locations could be constructed (in design and technology (D&T) lessons) or found. For example, a wood or jungle could be some bushes in the school grounds.

Activity 4: Each pair records their voices to accompany the talking story

This activity might need to be done on an individual computer with the support of a teaching assistant or parent helper. While it would be possible for each pair to record their voices in the computer suite, the level of background noise might make the recordings difficult if not impossible to hear. Also, the recordings will require the use of a microphone. Some laptop computers include a built-in microphone but most computers require an external microphone to be plugged in.

The pages which the children have created will have to be saved and transferred (e.g. by floppy disk, portable Universal Serial Bus (USB) drive or across the network) to the computer on which the recording is to be made. The method used to record the children's voices will be dependent on the way the software is designed to operate (see 'What do I need to know?', below).

Activity 5: The children evaluate the effectiveness of their talking story

Before the story is shown to the children, the various pages need to be brought together and linked (see 'What do I need to know?', below). The story is then ready for evaluation.

Remind the children of the similarities and differences between a talking story and a text-based story. You could demonstrate the completed talking story at this stage, or you could save this until they work on the computers in pairs.

The children need to decide how they will evaluate their talking story. At least three criteria should be identified. For example, the children may decide that the factors they are going to assess are:

⊙ How interesting the story is: Very – Quite – Not very – Not at all

⊙ How effective the illustrations are: Very – Quite – Not very – Not at all

⊙ Whether the story is better than if it had been presented
  on paper: Much – Quite – Not very – Not at all

The children then work through the story evaluating its success.

In a plenary discussion at the end of the lesson give the children an opportunity to share their evaluations with each other. In general terms they could be invited to suggest ways in which, were they to make another talking story, they could improve it.

What should the children know already?

What a talking story is and how it is structured

By the time the children reach Year 2, they will probably have used talking stories, though this cannot be taken for granted.

The features which you may wish to emphasise include:

- Talking stories have an author and an illustrator
- The text can be read aloud as often as the reader wishes
- Illustrations can be animated in some stories but not in all
- Just like a paper-based story, the story is told through a series of pages
- The talking story has a title page, a beginning, a middle and an ending
- The reader can move backwards and forwards through the story by clicking on a button to 'turn the page'
- Books are more portable and more convenient than computer-based talking stories

How to type simple text into a word processor or similar package

To help speed up the typing process, it is useful if the children are already familiar with the keyboard, particularly the use of the space bar and the **Shift** (⇧) key. The amount of typing required by each pair is fairly limited if the story content has been chosen carefully. Hence, this project could be used to introduce the children to entering text with a computer or to build upon introductory activities such as the writing of captions. The activities could be structured to emphasise the insertion of punctuation marks such as a full stop, comma, question mark or exclamation mark to reinforce sentence level work and extend the children's knowledge of the keyboard.

What resources will I need?

An example of a CD-ROM-based talking story

A basic talking story should be chosen to remind the children of the essential features of a talking story. Some talking stories can be quite lengthy and hence it might be necessary to select a couple of pages which model the use of text, images and the reading of the text particularly well. The talking stories featured in Project 1, provided on the CD-ROM accompanying this book, could be used as starting points for this project (see Project 1, 'What resources will I need?'). In addition, some examples of stories produced by children using *2Create A Story* (2Simple) are provided on the CD-ROM. These (or similar) could be used to help inspire the children when thinking about their own stories.

A Big Book of a story with a repetitive theme

Many picture books include text for young children which embodies a repetitive theme, thus encouraging the children to spot patterns in language and to enhance the book's predictability. This sort of repetition is useful in helping the children to devise their own talking story. Good examples include *Brown Bear, Brown Bear,*

What Do You See? (Martin and Carle 1995) or *We're Going on a Bear Hunt* (Rosen and Oxenbury 2001).

A program suitable for creating a talking story

The program used will clearly be dependent on what is available within the school. In addition to being able to enter text and insert images easily, the software will have to include some means of recording and/or playing sound files.

Dedicated story-making programs are the easiest to use – they have been designed specifically for use by children in creating talking stories. The two most well known are probably:

- ⊙ *2Create A Story* (2Simple) – http://www.2simple.com/2createastory/
- ⊙ *Storybook Weaver* (Riverdeep) – http://rivapprod2.riverdeep.net/portal/ page?_pageid=353,157846,353_157847&_dad=portal&_schema=PORTAL

Multimedia authoring packages all include these capabilities though some are easier to use than others. Those which are appropriate include:

- ⊙ *2Create* (2Simple) – www.2simple.com
- ⊙ *Kahootz* (Tag) – www.taglearning.com
- ⊙ *HyperStudio* (Tag) – www.taglearning.com
- ⊙ *Writer v3* (Granada) – www.onestopeducation.co.uk
- ⊙ *Junior MultiMedia Lab* (Sherston) – www2.sherston.com
- ⊙ *Kar2ouche* (Immersive Education) –www.immersiveeducation.com
- ⊙ *PowerPoint* (Microsoft) – see *PowerPoint in the classroom* at www.actden.com
- ⊙ *Open Office Impress* – www.openoffice.org

Most educational word processors read text aloud, but the children will gain more interest (and learn more) by recording and hearing their own voices. These can be recorded separately and added later (See 'What do I need to know?', below) but some word processors include their own sound-recording feature:

- ⊙ *Textease* (Softease) – www.softease.com
- ⊙ *Clicker* (Crick Software) – www.cricksoft.com

Included on the CD-ROM accompanying this book are some stories written by children in *Textease, Word* and *2Create* which you could use as examples. In addition there are *Textease* templates for simple branching stories. These include buttons interlinking the pages. You could give copies of these templates to more advanced groups of children to organise their own stories.

A computer that is less than four years old

While it is possible to create talking stories with a computer that is more than four years old, you might find it has insufficient memory or the processor is too slow to do the job effectively. Generally speaking, any computer built within four years of the publication of this book should be able to handle the tasks required for combining text, illustrations and sound.

What do I need to know?

How to structure a simple story with a repetitive theme

The more familiar you are with children's picture books, the more likely you are to be able to choose a story which is appropriate for the children you are teaching and specifically geared to the language skills you are aiming to develop. You can find information and advice on websites such as

⊙ Reading Is Fundamental (RIF) – www.rif.org.uk
⊙ Achuka – www.achuka.co.uk
⊙ Kids' Review – www.kidsreview.org.uk

How to enter text, images and sounds into the program

It is assumed that you will have the knowledge and skills needed to enter text and insert images, but many will be unfamiliar with recording digital sound clips and inserting these into a document. If you have a purpose-made program such as *2Create A Story* (2Simple) or *Storybook Weaver* (Riverdeep), then the process is very straightforward. But if you do not have one of these programs, the children can still record their voices using the **Sound Recorder** accessory which is provided with all PCs.

Recording a sound using the Sound Recorder accessory

All recent PCs include a basic sound-recording accessory as standard. This can be accessed by clicking on the **Start** menu and then selecting: **Accessories > Entertainment > Sound Recorder**.

To record your voice, click on the **Record** button (showing a large red dot). To stop recording, click on the **Stop** button (the black rectangle).

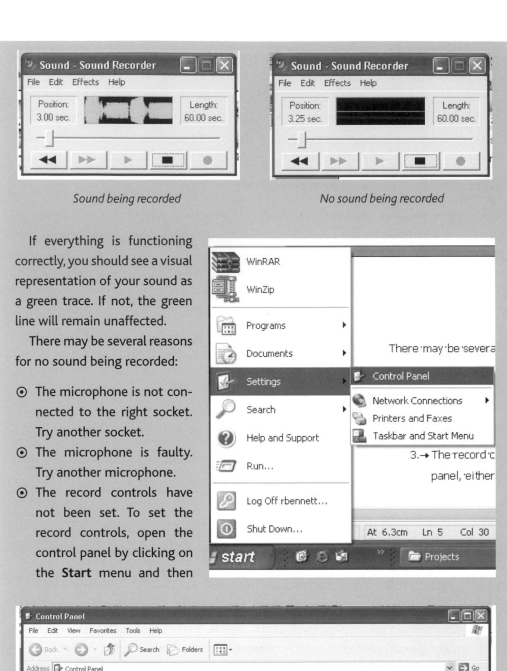

Sound being recorded   *No sound being recorded*

If everything is functioning correctly, you should see a visual representation of your sound as a green trace. If not, the green line will remain unaffected.

There may be several reasons for no sound being recorded:

⊙ The microphone is not connected to the right socket. Try another socket.

⊙ The microphone is faulty. Try another microphone.

⊙ The record controls have not been set. To set the record controls, open the control panel by clicking on the **Start** menu and then

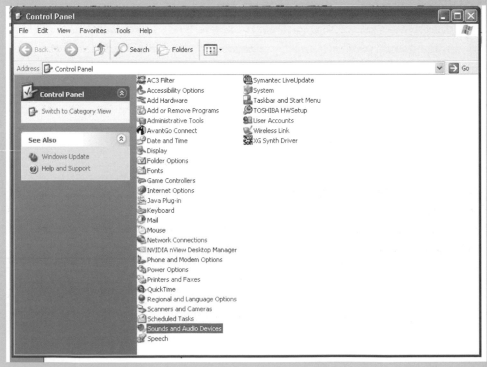

selecting **Settings > Control Panel.** Now double click on **Sounds and Audio Devices.** This will open the **Sounds** control panel. Click on the **Audio** tab and then on the **Sound recording > Volume** button:

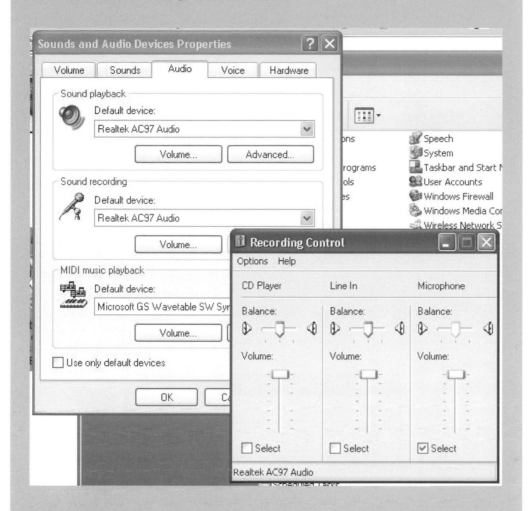

Move the volume slider control for the microphone to the top and make sure there is a tick in the **Select** box for the microphone. Close this window and then click on the **OK** button.

If none of the above works, then you should check with your technical support.

Once you have recorded your sound, save it where it can be found again using **Save As . . .,** from the **Edit** menu. A good place to save files is the **My Documents** folder.

Inserting a sound into a document

This will be largely dependent on the application you are using. The guide below shows you how to insert a sound into a *PowerPoint* document – most programs will follow a similar procedure.

⊙ When you have the relevant *PowerPoint* slide on the screen, click on **Insert > Movies and Sounds > Sound from File . . .** (NOTE: Recent versions of *PowerPoint* include a **Record Sound** feature similar to **Sound Recorder** shown above.)

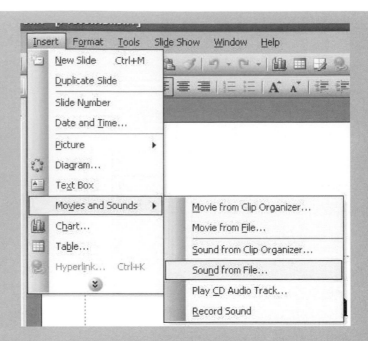

- Locate the sound file you want to insert and click on the **Insert** button. You will then be asked if you want the sound to play 'When Clicked' or 'Automatically' when the slide is viewed:

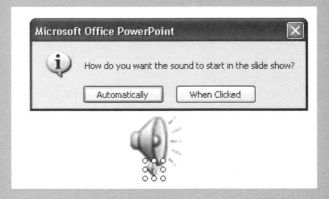

Recording a sound within a program

Again, the procedure for recording a sound is dependent upon the program you are using. The guide below uses *Textease* as an example. Other programs follow similar procedures.

- Once you have created the text and images on the page, double click on the object which you want the sound attached to.

- Click on the **Links** button on the menu bar at the top of the screen.

- Click on the **Action** tab.
- Click on the red button next to **Sound**.

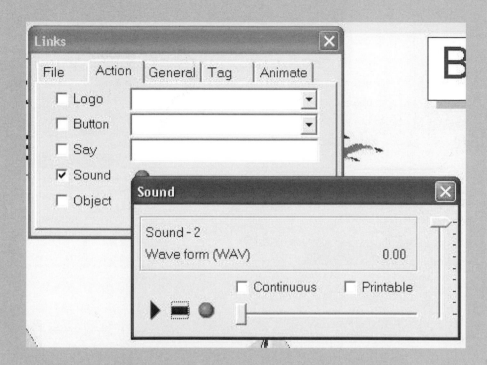

- Click the **Record** button and start recording the sound(s) required.
- Click the **Stop** button to finish the recording. (NOTE: The pointer on the right of the window should move up and down indicating the recording level. If it does not move, check for technical problems as indicated above.)
- Close the windows and click on the sound symbol to hear the sound.

(Optional) How to scan or import digital images into a computer and insert them into the program used for the story

Downloading images from a digital camera

The technicalities of downloading images from a digital camera vary considerably. In the main, provided the software which came with the camera is installed on your computer, the process is usually automatic once the camera is connected to the computer through a cable plugged into the computer's USB port. Most download programs ask the user to decide whether the pictures will be printed, saved or e-mailed. Clicking on the **Save** button should allow all or some of the images to be transferred from the camera to a folder (e.g. **My Photos** in **My Documents**). Once they have been saved they can be inserted into a document in the usual way.

Scanning or importing images into an art software package

Provided a scanner (or camera) has been connected appropriately, it is usually possible to directly transfer images from a scanner or import images from a webcam or digital camera. Below are instructions on how to import images into the *Paint* program which is one of the accessories which all PCs have installed as standard.

⊙ To open the *Paint* program, click on the **Start** menu and then go to **Programs > Accessories > Paint.**

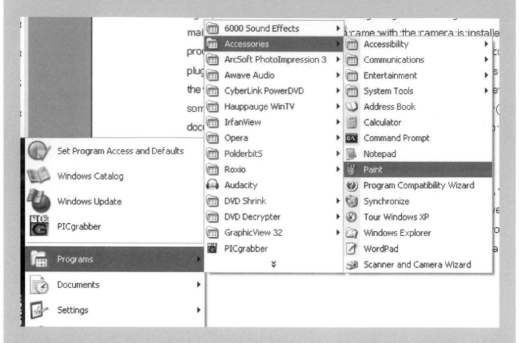

⊙ To scan an image directly into the *Paint* program or to create an image from a webcam you must firstly ensure that these are connected and switched on. Then select **From Scanner or Camera . . .** from the **File** menu:

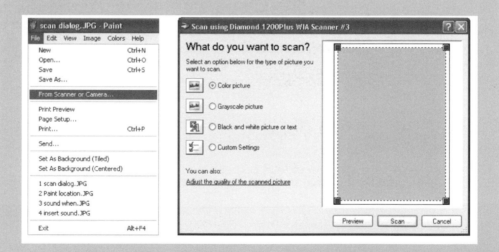

⊙ You should then be shown a dialogue box similar to that shown above (this will vary depending on the brand of scanner or webcam you have installed). The **Preview** button will allow you to check and, if necessary, adjust the area of the image to be scanned. The **Scan** button will scan an image of whatever is placed on the scanner platen (the glass surface similar to that of a photocopier) into the *Paint* program. Once scanned in, the image can be trimmed (or cropped) and saved.

⊙ It is advisable to save the image as a JPEG rather than a bitmap as bitmap images consume considerably more memory. After selecting **Save As . . .** from the **File** menu, change the type of file to **JPEG** by clicking on this on the **Save as type:** drop-down list:

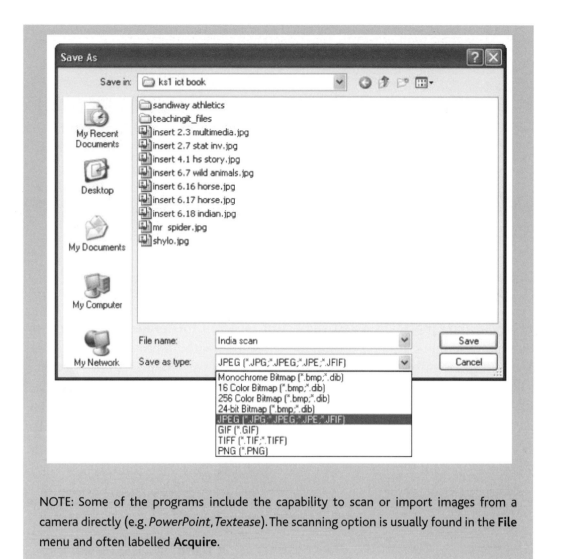

NOTE: Some of the programs include the capability to scan or import images from a camera directly (e.g. *PowerPoint, Textease*). The scanning option is usually found in the **File** menu and often labelled **Acquire**.

What will the children learn?

That computers can be used to manipulate text, images and sounds

That computer-based talking stories are written by authors and not computers

How to enter text, images and sounds into a computer

This activity not only enables children to become authors and illustrators in the traditional sense; it introduces them to the possibilities of multimedia authoring through the introduction of sound and interactivity.

Key vocabulary should be introduced as opportunities arise:

⊙ *Use of the mouse*: click, double click, right click, left click, drag, drop

⊙ *Entering text*: Shift, Caps Lock, backspace, delete, enter

⊙ *Manipulating images*: scan, crop (or trim), insert

⊙ *Manipulating sounds*: record, play, insert

⊙ *General computer terms*: text, image, sound, file, document, digitise

The additional component of sound not only reinforces their understanding of the way picture books work; it also emphasises the purpose of a story by reminding them that books are intended for readers. The children will immediately hear their recordings and may decide to rerecord their contribution. Sometimes they will recognise that the content of their written work could be enhanced with the addition of more emotive or descriptive words or phrases – or these could be suggested by the teacher or support assistant during the recording stage.

How to evaluate a piece of work completed on a computer and suggest improvements

The evaluation process is a very important aspect of this project. The identification of evaluation criteria is critical to the process; without criteria their analyses will be impressionistic and overly subjective. Clearly you will need to steer the children's discussions towards identification of criteria which are realistic and relevant, but you should be willing to include criteria which the children feel are very important, for example 'Is it colourful?'

The use of the rating scale helps to ensure that the criteria used are measurable. To obviate the children's conclusion that everything they have done is 'Very Good', use their criteria to evaluate a commercially produced talking story initially.

Challenging the more able and supporting the less able: modifying the project for older and younger pupils

Varying the responsibility for recording and inserting the sounds and images

Because the recording process is very straightforward for most software packages, some children could be given more control over the recording process. In addition, the children could decide whether they want to add sound effects to some of the objects on the screen. These could be recorded 'live'. The children gain a great deal of enjoyment in finding ways of replicating sounds, such as the sound of the wind or waves, or the trumpeting of an elephant.

Adjusting your expectation for the content for their pages

Story writing is an open-ended activity: some children will write copious amounts; others will produce very little. Because the talking story will become a very public presentation, attention can be legitimately placed on working with small 'chunks' of the story to improve its content and readability. This can be achieved through shared writing activities or by encouraging the children to discuss their contributions with each other.

Structuring the tasks to suit the needs of the children

If there are several children with little experience of using the computer or if the children lack confidence with writing, then you could prepare writing frames, template documents or word banks.

Writing frames

If some children are uncertain about writing their page of the story, they could be provided with a highly structured writing frame. For example, one pair's page might comprise two or three sentences with some missing words for them to complete:

> The ____ knocked loudly on the ____.
> 'Who is there?' asked the ____ nervously.

If the emphasis needs to be placed more on the entering of text than on the manipulation of images, then each frame could include a picture – either created by the teacher from Clip Art or downloaded from the internet. There are several websites which provide online picture books:

⊙ *Picture books* by Dandi Palmer – www.dandi.me.uk

⊙ *DreamBox StoryBox* – www.dreambox.com

Template documents

For stories with a strong repetitive composition, a template page could be provided for all the children. For example:

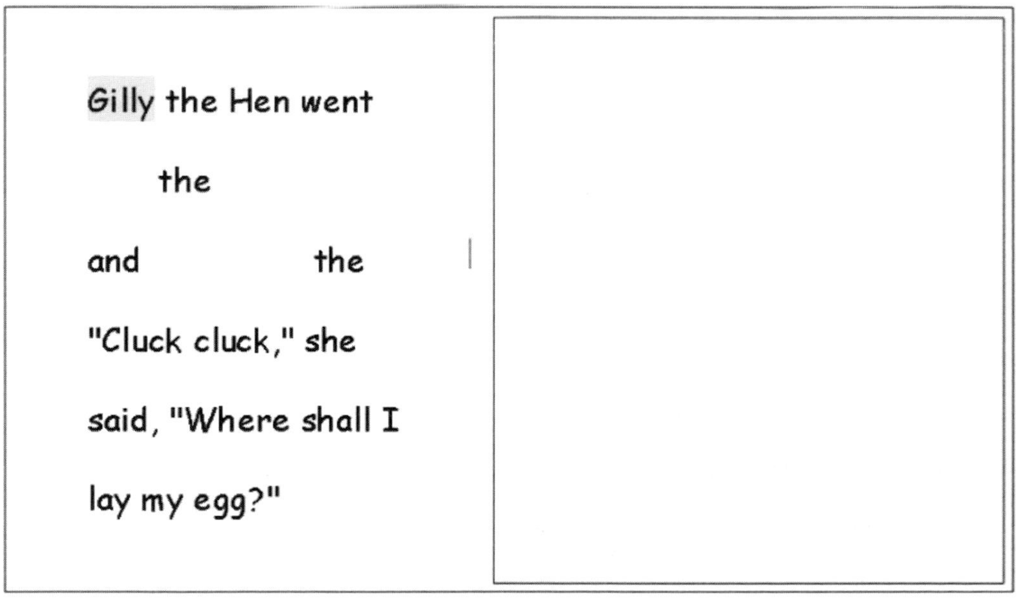

Gilly the Hen went
    the
and   the
"Cluck cluck," she
said, "Where shall I
lay my egg?"

Word banks

Different word banks could be created for the specific needs of children in the class. For example, in our *Gilly the Hen* story, the word bank might comprise prepositions and locations (see the CD-ROM accompanying this book for an example):

Varying the level of support

If classroom-based computers are used, then it will be possible to arrange for a support assistant to monitor and assist those working on the computers as the need arises. If the activity is conducted in a computer suite, then the activities will need to be carefully explained and demonstrated, with tasks being broken down into a series of sub-tasks and taught in sequence to ensure the children are given the guidance and support they need.

Another approach which is particularly useful when one or two classroom computers are being used in turn is for the activity to be explained initially to a pair of more experienced children who are then charged with the responsibility of instructing the next pair and so on.

In some settings, children in classes further up the school are used as 'buddies' to assist younger pupils in the computer lab. It is important that they are well briefed on their responsibilities and given strategies for the provision of support. For example, the 'expert' should never demonstrate but should explain and guide the inexperienced user through a process.

Why teach this?

It has been suggested that a word processor ought to be renamed a 'thought processor' or 'ideas organiser' (see Underwood and Underwood 1990: 125). Rather than simply using a word processor to present a tidied version of something which the children have drafted with a pencil and paper, they should be given the opportunity to draft, develop and design their page on screen. A useful guiding principle to bear in mind when using a word processor is that entering the text should be seen as the starting point for further work rather than the end-point.

The evaluation activity at the end of the project is very important in helping children to consider the impact of their work on others and to reinforce what they have learned – not only in terms of technical skill but also in reminding them of the decisions they made and the justifications for those decisions.

This project further develops particularly the final activity in QCA ICT Unit 2A: *Writing stories: communicating information using text* in which the children are asked to supply the missing text from a picture book. This project allows the children to become more creative and gain more experience of manipulating text by combining it with images and sounds.

ICT Unit 2B: *Creating pictures* is designed to complement the Art curriculum and hence the images which are created are not necessarily appropriate for book illustrations. However, the unit could be adapted to provide the children with skills and outcomes which could be used to produce images for their stories in this project.

This project could replace ICT Unit 3A: *Combining text and graphics* in its entirety, though if you feel greater emphasis needs to be placed on the manipulation of text, some of the short focused tasks in Unit 3A, such as replacing 'nice' with more expressive words, could be incorporated with this project.

By emulating a story and creating their own online version, the children will be engaging deeply with the structure, style and format of a picture book. Making decisions about characters and settings will enable them to appreciate the way that authors organise their work. The opportunities for the development of specific writing skills are considerable. The core activities in this project could be adapted depending on the learning needs of the children. For example, you could decide to focus primarily on the use of punctuation for effect or for the communication of direct speech. Alternatively, you may decide to use the story writing as a means of enhancing vocabulary through, for example, the use of word banks containing a wide range of imaginative vocabulary maybe suggested by the children in an initial brainstorming activity.

Because the children are writing their story for the class, they will need to consider the impact of their composition and the effect it might have on their audience. If the completed talking book is published on the school's website, then the potential audience could be world wide. The production of a class story provides the ideal context for shared writing activities. Reading from a book tends, in the main, to be a solitary activity. It has been shown (e.g. McFarlane 1997) that the computer screen encourages true collaboration over the content of written work far more effectively than paper-based activities. Children are more inclined to discuss and negotiate the words used when they are presented on a screen. This may have something to do with the ease with which changes can be made, though it might be argued that because the computer screen is similar to a television we are used to sharing what is presented with others. Sheingold *et al.* (1984) concluded that when working together at the computer the delineation of tasks is important – 'I'm the thinkist, you're the typist!'

This project links with *Humanities* Project 9 (*A video of a visit to a place of worship*) and *Arts* Project 6 (*Sound pictures*) which address similar learning objectives in other subject contexts.

References and further reading

Andrae, G. and Wojtowycz, D. (1997) *Rumble in the Jungle*, Dublin: O'Brien Press.

Carle, E. (2002) *The Very Hungry Caterpillar*, Harmondsworth: Puffin.

Hutchins, P. (2001) *Rosie's Walk*, London: Red Fox.

McFarlane, A. (1997) 'Thinking about writing', in McFarlane, A. (ed.) *Information Technology and Authentic Learning*, London: RoutledgeRoss.

McKee, D. (1996) *Not Now, Bernard*, London: Red Fox.

Martin, B. and Carle, E. (1995) *Brown Bear, Brown Bear, What Do You See?* Harmondsworth: Puffin.

Rosen, M. and Oxenbury, H. (2001) *We're Going on a Bear Hunt*, London: Walker Books.

Sheingold, K., Hawkins, J. and Carr, C. (1984) 'I'm the thinkist, you're the typist: the interaction of technology and the social life of classrooms', *Journal of Social Issues*, 40 (3), 49–61.

Underwood, J. and Underwood, G. (1990) *Computers and Learning: Helping Children Acquire Thinking Skills*, Oxford: Blackwell.

Project Fact Card: Project 3: Branching stories

Who is it for?

- 7- to 8-year-olds (NC Levels 2–3)

What will the children do?

- While reading an example of an interactive story, the children will make predictions about what will happen next and hence make decisions about what the character(s) in the story should do. Once they have appreciated the structure of a branching story, they will plan and create their own and then evaluate the outcome. Some children will make the links between pages in a branching story

What should the children know already?

- How to enter text and images into a word processor

What do I need to know?

- How to enter text and images into a word processor or presentation/web authoring package
- How to save pages from a word processor
- How to create a flow chart for a branching story
- How to create links between pages in a word processor (or multimedia/web authoring package)

What resources will I need?

- A word processor which includes the capability to make hyperlinks
- Alternatively, the project can be carried out with a multimedia presentation or authoring package
- At least one example of a simple branching story (or the first few pages of a branching story)
- A flow chart showing the structure of this example story

What will the children learn?

- How to reach collaborative decisions in the context of a branching story
- The structure and organisation of a branching story
- How to represent and plan a branching story as a flow chart
- (Some children) How to create links between pages in a word processor (or multimedia/web authoring package)

How to challenge the more able

- Use example stories which require more complex decision making (e.g. moral dilemmas)
- Give more responsibility to the children for planning the structure and content of the story

How to support the less able

- Provide writing frames or template stories
- Create a partially completed or skeleton story for completion by the children
- Structure the introductory activities more carefully to support the development of key skills and knowledge
- Provide more adult support

Why teach this?

- It addresses ICT NC KS2 PoS statements 2a, 3b
- It complements QCA ICT Scheme of Work Units 3A and 4A, and lays foundations for Unit 6A
- It addresses English NC KS2 PoS statements En1, 3a–f; En2, 5e; En3, 1a–e; En3, 2a–f
- It complements NLS units for Year 3 Term 1 Texts 9, 11, 15; Year 3 Term 2 Texts 6, 7; Year 3 Term 3 Texts 10, 11
- It provides an opportunity for meaningful collaborative work

Branching stories

Although the guidance provided here is focused on the needs of Year 3 children working at or around Levels 2–3, the activities, with modification, are also suitable for Years 2–6. The levels of intellectual demand can readily be adjusted through expectations, outcome and by adjusting the complexity and sophistication of the story flow chart. In addition, more responsibility for planning and implementation can be required of older or more experienced children.

What will the children do?

Activity 1: Reading and analysing an example of a branching story

Using an interactive whiteboard, data projector or large monitor, 'read' an example of a branching story with the class. Some endings could be left incomplete to encourage the children to offer their own suggestions.

Compare the advantages of this type of story over a conventional paper-based story. Emphasis could be placed on compositional features such as the use of vocabulary or textual features, for example setting and characterisation.

Show the flow chart for the story to the children. Ask if they can identify the routes they have already taken through the story. Another route through the story could be plotted on the flow chart which is then followed through in the story itself.

Conclude with a discussion about possible settings and plot lines for the class's own story.

Activity 2: Planning a whole-class branching story

This activity can be carried out with a blackboard, whiteboard, overhead projector and acetate sheet, flip chart, or separate sheets of A4 paper on a pinboard.

Discuss the children's suggestions for stories and focus on one which seems the most promising and the most appropriate. Ask for ideas as to how the story could start and select one. Jot this down then ask for two alternative options for the next

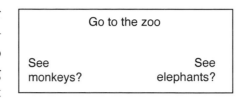

stage in the story. For example, the story could be about going to the zoo. The first decision might be to view the monkeys or the elephants. This could be represented on the first cell of the story flow chart as:

Now work on the next two options. For example, when seeing the monkeys, the decision could be to give them a banana or to pull faces at them. The decision when seeing the elephants could be to throw a stick at them or to throw them a piece of bread.

Show this in the flow chart – for example:

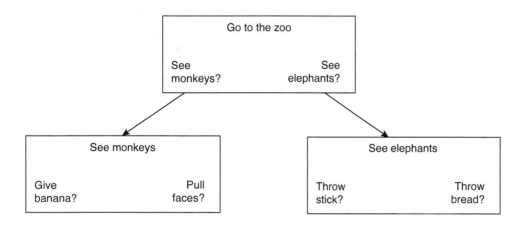

Continue building the story. Make sure that some choices lead to conclusions – for example, pulling faces could lead to being thrown out of the zoo. Throwing a stick could result in another visitor complaining and then being asked to leave.

The aim is to create sufficient scenes or pages for the children to be allocated one each or one between two, depending on the availability of computers and/or time. If, for example, the children have access to two classroom computers, a rota

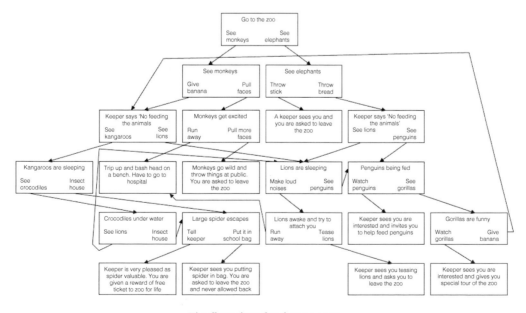

The flow chart for the zoo story

can be drawn up for pairs of children to write their contribution to the story. Alternatively, if there is access to a computer lab, the children could work on their contribution during two or three ICT lessons.

Activity 3: Writing the story

Using the flow chart as a starting point, the children work in pairs (or individually) to elaborate each page into an episode from the story. This intensive work on a small piece of text will provide opportunities for enhancing the quality of the writing through the addition of, for example, adjectives and adverbs. Your role at this point is to make suggestions, guide, advise and assist with the development of the text.

Activity 4 (optional extension): Illustrating the pages

The children could illustrate their 'pages' through the use of Clip Art images, digital photography, scanned drawings or digital images created with a computer-based art package. If there is access to digital video cameras, the children could even act out the scenes. (See Project 7 for more ideas.)

You decide to visit the Insect House. It is full of glass cases. In them are all sorts of insects. You are fascinated by the spiders. There are tarantulas, and a deadly Black Widow. One tank is labelled "South American Bird Eating Spider". The tank has pieces of bark and some exotic looking plants growing inside. You cannot see the spider anywhere. You are just about to move on to the next tank when you see an enormous brown hairy spider climbing down the outside of the tank. You love spiders and this one looks magnificent.

What will you do next?

Find a keeper and tell her the spider is escaping

Put the spider in your school bag quickly before anyone else

A page from the zoo story (produced using Textease)

Activity 5: Combining the pages into a single story

Once all the pages (or slides) have been completed they need to be brought together on one computer. If the school's computers are networked, this is a relatively straightforward procedure provided the children have saved their work in a shared area. Alternatively, you may need to save each of the children's pages on a floppy disk or portable USB 'pen' drive or memory stick and transfer them to a central computer.

Once the pages or slides have been compiled on one machine, the story can be test-read to check the pages make sense. This activity can form the basis for shared reading and writing as it might be necessary to change the content of some pages to aid continuity. If you have an interactive whiteboard and/or a projector and wireless keyboard, the rewriting process can be carried out collaboratively.

Links could be added at this stage by you or volunteers, but once this has been done for the first two or three pages, the process can become tedious and repetitive – better to demonstrate how this is done and then complete the linking outside the lesson (see Activity 5a).

Activity 5a: Linking the pages

Three possible ways this can be achieved are outlined below:

- *You complete the links.* This has the advantage of speed and reliability but the disadvantage that the children are not actively engaged in the process and hence a learning opportunity is missed.

- *Two pairs of enthusiastic computer users complete the links.* This ensures some involvement of the children and is a reliable approach – but not every child experiences the linking process.

- *Pairs take turns to add the links to their pages.* Best done on a classroom computer. This approach involves all the children (those with concluding pages can add a link back to the start of the story), but could lead to errors. Responsibility for training each pair in the linking process can be in the form of a relay – each outgoing pair training the incoming pair.

Activity 6: Evaluation of the story

The story in its finished form is demonstrated to the children and they are asked to decide on the criteria by which it will be evaluated. The criteria might be:

- Readability – are the pages easy to read?

- Interest – is the story interesting and exciting?

- Presentation – are the pages attractive and neatly arranged?

- Vocabulary – do the words used describe the situations and create tension?

- Choices – are the choices realistic and clearly communicated?

In pairs, the children read through the story a few times, taking different routes. They prepare a short report evaluating the story and its effectiveness.

The final plenary session provides an opportunity for each pair to report on their findings and to suggest ways in which their next story might be enhanced.

What should the children know already?

How to enter text and images into a word processor

This project could be used to build on the children's existing knowledge of entering text and images. Because the pages of text they will enter are focused and quite specific, there are opportunities to introduce different formatting effects. For example, keywords or phrases could be italicised for added effect; speech could be indented; and the choices presented at the foot of the page could be presented as a text box, an action button or a graphical button. Some presentation and multimedia packages allow the addition of sound effects. These could take effect as the page is opened or when a button is pressed.

What resources will I need?

A word processor which includes the capability to make hyperlinks

Most (but not all) word-processing packages now include the ability to make links to web pages and/or to other documents. Although this project can be completed to produce a paper-based adventure story bound into a book or displayed on a wall (the choices direct the reader to a particular page in the story), the exercise is more effective if hyperlinks are added to the pages so the linking is carried out on screen by the computer.

Alternatively, the activity can be carried out with a multimedia presentation or authoring package

Multimedia presentation and authoring packages are designed to link pages (or slides) together and allow the inclusion of text, images, sound, video and animation (i.e. multimedia). For this project, even the most basic presentation or multimedia authoring package will be sufficient.

At least one example of a simple branching story (or the first few pages of a branching story)

A flow chart showing the structure of this example story

Examples of these are provided on the CD-ROM which accompanies this book.

What do I need to know?

How to enter text and images into a word processor or presentation/web authoring package

Entering basic text into a word processor should be within the capabilities of most teachers and children. In some packages (e.g. *PowerPoint*), text can only be entered into a text box. In *PowerPoint*, a text box can be inserted from the **Insert** menu:

The mouse pointer changes to a 'cross hair' which, when dragged with the mouse button held down, will produce a text box, into which can be typed text. The text box can be dragged and reshaped to fit around pictures and buttons placed on the slide.

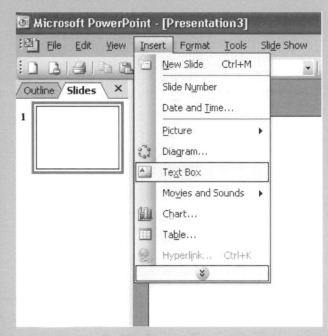

Text boxes are created automatically in *Textease* by simply clicking on the screen and typing. Once the text has been entered, the text box can be resized and moved by double clicking to highlight the box and then dragging. (NOTE: To resize the textbox in *Textease* without resizing the text font, click on the edge of the box rather than the 'handles' in the corner.)

How to save pages from a word processor

While this might sound like a very basic skill, some word processors and networks have difficulty creating links to files or documents if spaces have been included in the file name. To obviate potential problems, you and the children should avoid using spaces and punctuation marks when saving the pages. Give the pages names such as **Page1**, **Page2** or **Page_1**, **Page_2**.

How to create a flow chart for a branching story

This can be achieved in a variety of ways:

⊙ *A large sheet of paper, whiteboard or blackboard*. The boxes and links are added freehand as the story progresses.
⊙ *A4 sheets of paper and a pinboard*. The various episodes in the story are summarised on each A4 sheet and posted up in their relative positions on the pinboard.
⊙ *An interactive whiteboard and a drawing package or flow-charting package*. It is possible to create the flow chart on a computer, but sometimes the technicalities of

creating the boxes and entering the text can slow down the process. However, the advantage is that all the children can have a printout of the storyboard when completed.

How to create links between pages in a word processor (or multimedia/web authoring package)

For most Microsoft Office programs (e.g. *Word*, *PowerPoint*, *Publisher*), hyperlinks are inserted into a document by highlighting the piece of text (i.e. dragging over it) or by selecting the object (i.e. by clicking on it once) and then choosing the **Hyperlink** . . .

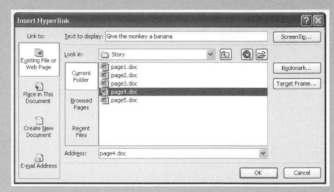

option from the **Insert** menu.

This will then produce a dialogue box from which can be chosen the page to which the link will be made.

In *Granada Writer v3*, the links are made by highlighting the text or selecting an object and then clicking on the **Links** button.

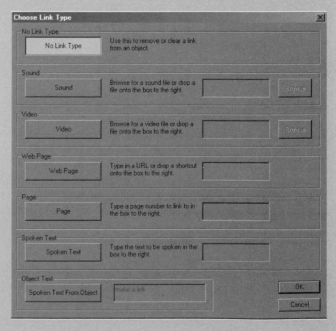

This will bring up the **Links** dialogue box from which can be selected the relevant page, web page, sound, video, or spoken/ object text.

For making links from other word-processing or presentation packages, refer to the handbook that accompanies the software or on-screen help.

What will the children learn?

How to reach collaborative decisions in the context of a branching story

When coming to joint decisions, children need to be coached or trained in how to take account of each other's viewpoints before reaching a consensus view (see 'Why teach this?', below).

The structure and organisation of a branching story

How to represent and plan a branching story as a flow chart

The flow chart for branching stories can form a symmetrical pattern or the pages can be interlinked in a highly complex way. The example story shown in Activity 2 shows only two decisions per page but the number of decisions can vary – though this can make the flow charting difficult. The number of conclusions can also vary according to the ways in which the story is organised.

(Some children) How to create links between pages in a word processor (or multimedia/web authoring package)

As indicated above (see What do I need to know?), hyperlinking can be done by the children themselves providing this aspect is carefully organised, otherwise the links may not work.

Challenging the more able and supporting the less able: modifying the project for older and younger pupils

Adjusting the level of decision making involved

Kate's Choice (see www.thinkingtogether.org.uk) is an example of a story in which the children have to help Kate decide what to do when her best friend confesses to stealing a box of chocolates from the sweet shop as a present for his mother. The decision making is quite complex owing to conflicts in loyalty to a friend, and being honest. Many issues associated with PSHE (personal, social and health education) could lead to the production of stories with an added moral or health and safety dimension.

For those needing more support, the decision making could be restricted through, for example, scaffolding the activities more carefully or providing template stories in which the decisions have already been made in the opening discussion.

Adjusting the level of responsibility for planning the structure and content of the story

If you feel there is a group of children who are sufficiently skilled and reliable, the activity can be organised as group work – with each group taking responsibility for the planning, organisation and writing of their own stories.

Children who are less experienced in using a word processor or those who need more support for structuring their writing will probably benefit from a writing frame or a template document. For example:

> You decide to
>
>
>
> When you

For those children who need additional support, a skeleton page can prove beneficial. The episode for their contribution to the story is provided for them as a document with the barest outline of the story. For example:

> You go to see the monkeys. They are doing funny things. One of them comes to the bars and puts its hand out.
>
> What will you do?
>
>
> Give the monkey a banana   Pull faces at the monkey

You go to see the monkeys. There are five in the cage. They are doing funny things. A big brown monkey is hanging upside down by its tail and making very loud noises. A little monkey is eating an apple with its feet. A big fat monkey comes to the bars and puts its hand out.

What will you do?

| Give the monkey a banana | Pull faces at the monkey |

If you are uncertain about the interests, experience or capabilities of the children with whom you will be working, you could produce a partially completed story (e.g. the first three pages) to spark off their interest or to ensure that the context for the story is one which fits in with the main theme for the class, or even with the Clip Art which you know is available for them to use in the story.

Adjusting the level of demand of the tasks

If the children are inexperienced with the software you are using – for example, you may decide to use *PowerPoint* with them for the first time – you should structure the introductory activities more carefully to ensure that they acquire the skills they need. The first activity in the computer suite might be for them to all create a very similar title page which includes some text and a picture. Once they have followed your directions in creating this common page, they could then be given the outline content for their own page(s) and use their newly acquired skills to create it.

Adjusting the level of support

A teaching assistant or a parent helper who feels sufficiently confident is a great asset in the computer suite when doing this type of activity. The teaching assistant can focus his/her attention on those who need either technical or language support to get the most from the activities.

It is also possible for children to support each other through peer support. This might require the establishment of a set of procedures which are familiar to the children. For example:

If I need help:

1. Try something out myself.

2. Ask my partner if s/he can work out what to do.

3. Ask the people working at the computer next to me.

4. Try the help screen.

5. Ask the teacher.

Why teach this?

Because the children are working intensively on a short piece of writing which contributes to a larger whole, they need to think carefully about the way the information on the page is presented and the effect it will have on their intended audiences. Year 3 children, and certainly those who are older, are more than capable of discussing the impact of their written work on the reader, and how a change of phraseology can influence the choice the reader might take – for example, compare '*Will you run away?*' with '*Will you run away and hide?*'

Some children could be shown how to add sound effects to their buttons – particularly if they are using a package which supports multimedia such as *Granada Writer v3* or *PowerPoint*.

The evaluation session and the subsequent plenary discussion provide plenty of opportunity for children to engage in meaningful self- and peer evaluation of their work.

When completing QCA ICT Unit 3A: *Combining text and graphics*, rather than producing a class magazine, the children could produce a class branching story. The skills needed are broadly the same although the illustrations in a story accompany it rather than convey specific information. As an alternative to writing the newspaper article in Unit 4A: *Writing for different audiences*, the children could produce a branching story centred on a theme or topic related to their other class work. They could choose to target their story on a parallel class or another age group within the school – and could possibly e-mail the other class or create a small questionnaire to poll the views of the other class on the focus for the story. By having a clearly defined audience in mind, the writing should be more focused and they will have the opportunity to receive real feedback on the effectiveness of their efforts.

Often, children have mastered most of the basic techniques of word processing (entering and formatting text, inserting and manipulating images) by Year 3 and teachers have difficulty in finding activities which extend or challenge the children's capabilities. Creating simple branching stories with text, images and hyperlinks lays the foundation for later multimedia work with combining sound, video and animation effects. The concept of hyperlinking is fundamental to multimedia and hence will provide valuable prior experience for Unit 6A: *Multimedia presentation.*

Brainstorming is an important component in planning a branching story. Although the structure for the story could be decided by the teacher beforehand, the children become more engaged in the process if they feel the story has been designed and created collaboratively. The style of writing for a branching story is slightly unusual as it is written in the second person – for example '*You decide to visit the monkeys. What will you do next?*' It is similar to instructional writing (e.g. recipes) but provides the children with an opportunity to use this style of writing in an imaginary context. Because this activity focuses on the production of a specific form of story, the children will need to work within a tight structure to ensure the outcome is not only interesting but also coherent – the various episodes need to be self-contained but also link with what precedes and follows in the narrative. Whereas conventional stories can be written without a plan, planning is of critical importance to branching stories.

Plotting episodes in a familiar story can be a preliminary or a follow-on exercise. Branching stories can arise by taking a well-known story, such as *Cinderella,* and deciding what might have happened at various points in the story. For example, what if Cinderella had refused to clean the house? What if she had not danced with the prince; not worn the glass slipper; if the slipper had broken as it fell from her foot; if she had continued dancing when the clock struck midnight; etc.

Some fascinating research by Rupert Wegerif and Lynn Dawes (e.g. Dawes and Wegerif 1998) has indicated that computer-based branching stories can prove valuable in helping children develop and use thinking skills. They suggest that when working collaboratively children engage in different types of talk, the most productive of which in terms of developing their thinking is 'Exploratory Talk'. To achieve this they suggest the children devise a set of class rules for collaborative talk. For example:

Our talking rules

⊙ We share our ideas and listen to each other

⊙ We talk one at a time

⊙ We respect each other's opinions

⊙ We give reasons to explain our ideas

⊙ If we disagree we ask 'why?'

⊙ We try to agree in the end

(Wegerif and Dawes 2004: 25)

To find more information about Exploratory Talk, see www.mape.org.uk or www.thinkingtogether.org.uk

See also *Humanities* Project 3 (*Using an information source*) and *Science* Project 4 (*Branching databases*) for related activities.

References and further reading

Dawes, L. and Wegerif, R. (1998) 'Encouraging exploratory talk: practical suggestions', Newman College, *MAPE Focus on Literacy*, Autumn 1998. http://www.mape.org.uk/curriculum/english/exploratory.htm (accessed 19/9/02).

Wegerif, R. and Dawes, L. (1988) 'Encouraging exploratory talk around computers', in M. Monteith (ed.) *IT for Learning Enhancement*, Exeter: Intellect Books.

Wegerif, R. and Dawes, L. (2002) 'Talking solutions: the role of oracy in the effective use of ICT', in M. Monteith (ed.) *Teaching Primary Literacy with ICT*, Buckingham: Open University Press.

Wegerif, R. and Dawes, L. (2004) *Thinking and Learning with ICT: Raising Achievement in Primary Classrooms*, London: Routledge Falmer.

Project Fact Card: Project 4: Working with audio

Who is it for?

- 6- to 8-year-olds (NC Levels 2–3)

What will the children do?

- After listening to and evaluating an audio dramatisation of a short story, the children will plan and script their own audio play. They will record and/or edit sound effects and then record and edit their audio play. Finally, they will evaluate their own and others' audio plays

What do I need to know?

- How to use an audio tape recorder
- How to format a playscript with a word processor
- How to record sounds on a computer and save them
- How to edit sounds using **Sound Recorder**
- How to play back sounds on a computer
- (Optional) How to find sound effects on the internet

What should the children know already?

- How to use an audio tape recorder
- The structure of a simple playscript
- Basic word processing (entering text and editing)

What resources will I need?

- At least one audio cassette recorder (more if available) with microphone
- Audio cassette tapes
- A microphone connected to a computer
- An audio dramatisation on tape or CD
- A CD player
- Sound effects and music CDs
- **Sound Recorder** accessory package
- (Optional) A computer with internet access

What will the children learn?

- How to use the formatting features of a word processor to present a playscript (including sound effects)
- How to record and check an audio recording
- How to evaluate a sound recording and suggest improvements
- (Optional) How to record and edit sounds with a simple sound-editing software package

How to challenge the more able

- Give more responsibility for planning and organising the project
- A more challenging context for the sound play
- Record and edit the play using a sound-editing software package

How to support the less able

- Provide a skeleton structure for the playscript
- Provide writing frames and/or word banks
- Provide more support through adults or peers

Why teach this?

- It addresses ICT NC KS2 PoS statements 2a, 3a, 3b
- It complements QCA ICT Scheme of Work Units 3B, 4A
- It addresses English NC KS2 PoS statements En1, 1b, 1c, 4a, 4b, 4d, 9b, 11a–c; En2, 4h, 4i, 8g; En3, 1a–e, 2a–c, 2f, 12
- It complements NLS units for Year 3 Term 1 Texts 3, 4, 5, 14; Year 3 Term 2 Text 5
- It extends ICT capability into challenging and rewarding areas

Working with audio

The project described here has Year 3 children in mind, but the activities could readily be adapted for any age group. For younger children, such as those in Year 2, the activities may need to be structured more carefully – or the playscript could be written by the whole class as a shared writing activity. Older or more experienced children will gain a great deal by exploring the digital sound-editing software and creating their own sound effects by combining and/or modifying those which already exist.

What will the children do?

Activity 1: Listen to and evaluate an audio dramatisation of a short story

Depending on the story being dramatised (see 'What resources will I need?', below), you might decide to read them the story first, or to hear the dramatisation and then read the relevant story or chapter.

A follow-up discussion should focus on the similarities and differences between the story and its dramatisation. You could draw the children's attention to:

Similarities

⊙ The characters, settings and plot are broadly similar

⊙ Some of the characters' speeches/dialogue are the same

⊙ The duration is about the same

Differences

⊙ Different actors take on the roles of the characters

⊙ There is (or is not) a narrator to provide background information

⊙ There is music and/or sound effects

Finally, tell them they are going to record their own radio play similar to that which they have heard. It could be based on a story with which they are familiar (e.g. a well-known fairy tale such as *Goldilocks and the Three Bears*), a story or chapter which you read to them, or (if you feel the children are sufficiently imaginative) a story of their own.

Activity 2: Plan and script an audio play

Before attempting to write their own playscript, the children will need to gain some familiarity with the structure, format and style of writing of this genre. If you have multiple copies of a playscript, the children will be able to read through their own copy with you; an alternative is to project or produce an enlarged photocopy of an extract for them to see and discuss. In addition to drawing attention to the format of the script, you should also mention the stage directions. It is unlikely you will find an example which includes sound effects, but you might discuss how the scene being studied could be enhanced for a listening audience with the addition of background sounds and sound effects to help the visualisation of unseen actions.

For example, here is an extract from a script for *Goldilocks and the Three Bears* (reproduced with permission from Brian Wakeling: http://freespace.virgin.net/b.wakeling/Writing/scripts.html):

GOLDILOCKS AND THE THREE BEARS

SET: TABLE, THREE CHAIRS, AND THREE BEDS. BOWLS OF PORRIDGE AND A JUG OF MILK ON TABLE. EXITS AT BOTH SIDES. BABY BEAR, MUMMY BEAR, AND DADDY BEAR ARE SEATED AT THE TABLE.

D Bear: Tuck in, everybody!

BABY BEAR IS THE FIRST TO TAKE A SPOONFUL

B Bear: Ouch! That's too hot!
M Bear: Is it dear? *[SHE TAKES A SPOONFUL]* Ooh! Yes, it is hot.

DADDY BEAR LAUGHS

D Bear: Oh, nonsense! Porridge can never be too hot! *[HE TAKES A SPOONFUL]* Aaargh! Water, water, quick!

HE JUMPS UP AND RUSHES AROUND FRANTICALLY TRYING TO FIND SOME WATER, WHILST CLAWING AT HIS THROAT. HE EVENTUALLY GRABS THE MILK JUG WITH BOTH HANDS AND DRINKS DIRECTLY FROM IT.

D Bear: Aaah! That's better!

This script is intended for a live stage performance. For an audio play it would need to be adapted to describe sound effects, as below:

GOLDILOCKS AND THE THREE BEARS

MUSIC:	*Teddy Bears' Picnic*
FX:	*Mummy Bear humming*
FX:	*Porridge ladled into bowls*
FX:	*Sound of scraping chairs*
D Bear:	Thank you Mummy Bear. That porridge looks delicious. Tuck in, Baby Bear, while it is still warm!
FX:	*Baby Bear dipping spoon into porridge and slurping*
B Bear:	Ouch! That's too hot!
M Bear:	Is it dear?
FX:	*Mummy Bear dipping spoon into porridge and slurping*
M Bear:	Ooh! Yes, it is hot.

DADDY BEAR LAUGHS

D Bear:	Oh, nonsense! Porridge can never be too hot!
FX:	*Daddy Bear dipping spoon into porridge and slurping*
D Bear:	Aaargh! Water, water, quick!
FX:	*Daddy Bear knocking over chair and rushing around room*
FX:	*Glug Glug as Daddy Bear drinks from jug*
D Bear:	Aaah! That's better!

At this point, decide whether you want all the children to adapt the same script, (which you could provide as a word processor file) or whether you want them to produce their own script from scratch.

The following strategies could be adopted to ensure that the children have sufficient time to achieve a productive outcome:

⊙ All children work on the same story but each group tackles a different scene.

⊙ Give the children a brief incident to dramatise (e.g. coming home late for tea, sorting out a playground disagreement, trying to persuade a parent to do something).

⊙ Ask the children to produce only the first page of a script – which might be extended later.

⊙ Provide a 'skeleton' script (or series of scripts) which the children can elaborate and extend.

⊙ Use a picture book as the basis for the play and allocate one page to each group for adaptation.

Before letting the children word process their scripts it is advisable to ensure they know how to set out the script. They may need to be instructed in how to use bold and italic and how to use the tab key to align their paragraphs (see 'What do I need to know?', below). If all the groups are working on the same story, you could take them step by step through the first two or three lines of the story, demonstrating the techniques they will need.

Activity 3: Record and/or edit sound effects

Making and recording sound effects

Once the scripts have been written the children will need to produce a list of the sound effects they require. If all the children are working on adaptations of the same story, then the sound effects needed are likely to be the same or at least very similar. In this case, the effects could be recorded as a whole-class lesson – with different children (or pairs) assigned to producing each effect.

When the sound recordings are being made there will need to be absolute silence as the microphone will pick up any background noise. Although the sounds could be recorded on a tape recorder, recording them into a computer will give far greater control (see 'What do I need to know?', below).

If groups are working on different stories or episodes from the same story, then the sound effects needed might be quite diverse. This could be organised as a whole-class lesson (as above), but could also be organised as group work under the supervision of a teaching assistant or parent helper, with the computer located where background noise can be kept to a minimum.

Editing sound effects

If time and technical confidence permits, the children could work with a simple sound-editing software package to edit their own sound effects. This will require the use of headphones to enable the children to preview their own sound effects without disturbing the rest of the class (see 'What do I need to know?', below, for technical guidance).

Activity 4: Record and edit an audio play

The organisation of this activity will be dependent on the number of groups and the time which is available. The recording could be made by each group in front of the whole class. This could be spread out over the period of a week, using, for example, the last session of each day. Alternatively, the groups could go to a separate 'quiet' area in turn to record their scene under the supervision of an adult.

Activity 5: Evaluate their own and others' audio plays

Once the recordings have been made, the children need to hear and evaluate their own and each other's performances. An evaluation sheet could be devised in collaboration with the children. The criteria for evaluation might include the following:

Name of play:			
Content	Very	Quite	Not
The scene was interesting			
The scene was entertaining			
The story was well told			
Dramatic	Very	Quite	Not
The acting was convincing			
The voices were clear			
Technical	Very	Quite	Not
The sound effects were appropriate			
The recording was clear			

The children will have to understand that they will need to justify where they have put their ticks – particularly explaining how improvements could be made.

What should the children know already?

How to use an audio tape recorder

At least one child in each group needs to know how to operate the tape recorder. He/She needs to know how to record, rewind and play back in case part of a scene needs to be rerecorded.

The structure of a simple playscript

This could be taught in the context of this activity, but familiarity with the way simple playscripts are organised will enable the children to appreciate the need for describing the sound effects needed for an audio version.

Basic word processing (entering text and editing)

By Year 3 children should be able to enter text, using the **Shift** key for capitalisation and punctuation. They will also need to know how to change the format to italic and bold and how to use the tab key to align the dialogue. If the children are unfamiliar with these techniques, then an introductory task should be included in Activity 2.

What resources will I need?

At least one audio cassette recorder (more if available) with microphone

Some cassette recorders have built-in microphones but will allow for an external mike to be connected. An external microphone is preferable as internal mikes tend to pick up the noise of the motor driving the tape mechanism.

Audio cassette tapes

Preferably each group should have their own, suitably labelled.

A microphone connected to a computer

Most computers will include a socket for a microphone (on many computers the headphones socket is coloured green and the microphone socket is red or pink). A mike for a computer can be purchased for as little as £10.00 from most computer shops.

An audio dramatisation on tape or CD

The BBC has produced a range of audio recordings, some of which are fully dramatised radio plays (e.g. *Paddington Bear*). Go to the BBC online shop (www. bbcshop.com/).

A CD player

This might be needed if the dramatisation has been recorded on CD. However, most computers will play audio CDs and, provided the volume can be turned up high enough, will be sufficient.

Sound effects and music CDs

Sounds effects and music on CDs are saved in a format which some editing pro-grams (e.g. *Audacity*) cannot handle, though the tracks can be 'ripped' from the CD and saved onto the computer, thereby enabling a library of effects and music clips to be compiled for use by the children. It must be remembered, however, that commercially produced music and sound effects CDs are subject to copyright restrictions.

Sound Recorder accessory package

Sound Recorder is a utility program which comes as standard on PCs. It is found by clicking on *Start > Programs > Accessories > Entertainment > Sound Recorder*.

(Optional) A computer with internet access

Sound effects can be readily located and downloaded from the internet. One of the best sources of free sound files is http://www.findsound.com

What do I need to know?

How to use an audio tape recorder

It is assumed that you will know the basics of operating a cassette recorder. However, the following advice might be useful:

- ⊙ Encourage the children to use the *pause* button rather than the *stop* button. Using the *stop* button tends to lead to clicks and clunks being recorded.
- ⊙ Better quality tapes lead to better quality recordings.

How to format a playscript with a word processor

Although most people are familiar with formatting text (using italic, bold, underline, etc.) some may not be aware of the use of tab controls.

Setting indent controls in *MS Word*
Firstly, ensure the ruler is visible at the top of the document.

If it is not, click on **Ruler** in the **View** menu.

The margins can be moved by dragging the blue bands on the edges of the ruler. By dragging the lower part of the left-hand text marker, a 'hanging indent' can be created. This means the  first line of each paragraph will start at the first marker and subsequent lines will start at the second mark:

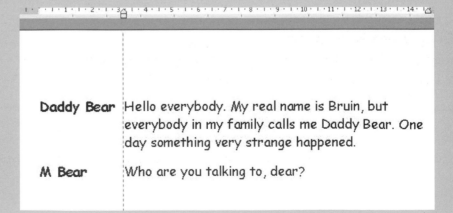

Daddy Bear	Hello everybody. My real name is Bruin, but everybody in my family calls me Daddy Bear. One day something very strange happened.
M Bear	Who are you talking to, dear?

Also, if you tap the tab key (usually on the left of the keyboard above the **Caps Lock** key), after typing in the name of the character, the text will be entered in line with the second marker without the need to type spaces to fill the gap.

How to record sounds on a computer and save them

For detailed instructions on using the **Sound Recorder** accessory provided as standard on all PCs, refer to 'What do I need to know?' in Project 2.

How to edit sounds using **Sound Recorder**

NOTE: Short video tutorials demonstrating how to use **Sound Recorder** are provided on the CD-ROM accompanying this book. These could be used by you and/or the children when learning how to record and edit sound recordings.

Combining two or more sounds

Two or more sounds can be combined. For example, you might want three boing sounds for Daddy Bear's bed. Record and save one boing sound (e.g. by twanging a ruler). Then click on the **Edit** menu and select **Insert file . . .**

Locate the boing sound file which you have just saved and click **Open**. The saved boing will be inserted before the boing which has just been recorded. This new file can be saved as *Boing2*. The new sound will be inserted at the point at which the existing sound has been stopped. It is possible therefore to insert a sound in the middle of another sound.

Merging two or more sounds

Notice also that two (or more) sounds can be mixed. A boing sound could be mixed with a creaking sound. The two sounds will be overlaid or superimposed upon each other. Try experimenting.

Deleting unwanted sounds from a recording

The boing sound which I recorded included a short gap before the sound played: the time delay between me clicking the *record* button and twanging a ruler. This silent section at the start of the sound can be removed (or 'edited out').

Listen to the sound a few times to see more or less where the silence ends. Then move the slider (by dragging with the mouse pointer) to the start of the sound. Pressing *play* will enable you to check you are in the correct position in the recording – also the green display will show where the sound starts.

Then, from the **Edit** menu, select **Delete Before Current Position**, and the unwanted silence will be deleted.

How to play back sounds on a computer

If your computer does not have a copy of *Windows Media Player* installed, then it can be downloaded free of charge from the Microsoft website: http://www.microsoft.com/windows/windowsmedia/

(Optional) How to find sound effects on the internet

Some search engines such as AltaVista (http://www.altavista.com) have a search facility for sounds.

See also: http://www.findsounds.com

Once the desired sound has been located, right click on the file and use **Save Target As . . .** to save it onto your computer.

What will the children learn?

How to use the formatting features of a word processor to present a playscript (including sound effects)

As indicated above, there are several sub-skills which the children will need:

⊙ Entering text from a keyboard

⊙ Entering text from a word bank (for those who need additional support)

- Using the **Shift** key for capitalisation and punctuation

- Highlighting, copying and pasting text

- Formatting text for emboldening, italicising and underlining

- Using the tab key to align text

These can be taught through the context of the activities or could be structured into short, focused tasks at the start of the lesson(s). In addition, the children may need to be reminded about saving, loading and printing documents.

How to record and check an audio recording

Most children will know how to use an audio tape recorder but you may need to demonstrate some of the features they may not have used, such as resetting the tape counter. The sub-skills needed for operation of the tape recorder include:

- Inserting and removing the tape

- Using the play and rewind buttons

- Using the record button

- Setting the tape counter to zero and using this to cue playback and recording

How to evaluate a sound recording and suggest improvements

Evaluation is more effective if it is guided by criteria, particularly if the criteria have been defined by the children themselves. The children may need to be advised on how to give feedback and how to make constructive suggestions. If an evaluation session is not carefully managed, it can lead to negative and personal responses.

(Optional) How to record and edit sounds with a simple sound-editing software package

Sound Recorder is very easy to use but has limitations. The trickiest part of the process is making sure the sound files are saved with relevant names in a known folder so they can be found again.

The basic sub-skills needed for using **Sound Recorder** are:

- Loading and running the program

- Making sure the microphone is connected and working

- Checking the sound levels

- Using the on-screen record, rewind and play buttons

- Saving finished sound file with a relevant name in a known folder

- Starting a new recording by clicking on **New** in the **File** menu

More advanced skills needed for editing sound files include:

⊙ Adjusting the volume

⊙ Adjusting the duration of a sound clip

⊙ Adding echoes to a sound clip

⊙ Using the slider to position the edit point

⊙ Deleting unwanted sounds or silences

⊙ Combining two sound clips

⊙ Merging two sound clips

If you want the children to experiment with sound recordings, you could set them a focused task using sound files which you (or they) have created earlier.

Challenging the more able and supporting the less able: modifying the project for older and younger pupils

Adjusting the level of responsibility for planning and organising the project

Some groups may need less support than others and could be given far more responsibility for organising their own activities. Some children may be willing and able to develop sound recordings on their home computers. This could be encouraged but it should be remembered that this might disadvantage those children without access to a computer.

   Those requiring more support will need the activities to be more carefully structured. For example:

Provide a skeleton structure for the playscript

GOLDILOCKS AND THE THREE BEARS

MUSIC: *Teddy Bears' Picnic*
FX:
D Bear: This porridge looks _____. Eat it all up Baby Bear.
FX:
B Bear: OUCH!
M Bear: What is the matter, Baby Bear?
B Bear: My _____ is _____.

Provide writing frames and/or word banks
A writing frame could be used to act as a framework for the children's writing. For example, the following could be provided for some groups as an initial activity to help them understand how to structure a playscript on screen.

```
┌─────────────────────────────────────────────────────────────────┐
│              GOLDILOCKS AND THE THREE BEARS                       │
│                                                                   │
│   MUSIC:    Teddy Bears' Picnic                                   │
│   FX:       Mummy Bear slopping porridge into three bowls         │
│   D Bear:                                                         │
│   FX:       Baby Bear slurps porridge                             │
│   B Bear:                                                         │
│   M Bear:                                                         │
│   FX:       Mummy Bear slurping porridge                          │
│                                                                   │
└─────────────────────────────────────────────────────────────────┘
```

If this is combined with a series of missing phrases in a word bank, then the children who lack confidence should be sufficiently supported.

Specifying the content for the sound play

Some stories have greater potential for background sound effects than others. For example, a story set at the seaside provides more opportunity than one set in a house. More obscure settings (e.g. a haunted house, an alien planet) will inevitably require more complex and convoluted sound effects than familiar settings (the playground, the classroom, a house). If you have a set of sound effects to hand, you may decide to influence the children's choice of story to reflect this.

Recording and editing the play using a sound-editing software package

If sufficient memory is available, the whole play could be recorded on a computer. In this case, the dialogue could be recorded initially without sound effects and then the sound effects could be merged with the dialogue at relevant intervals. There is, however, no 'undo' facility in **Sound Recorder** and so the children will need to save their recording before each change is made. This will make the process quite complicated.

If the children (and you) are sufficiently confident, the whole play could be edited with *Audacity* (**Sound Forge**). This includes an 'undo' facility but is a more complex package.

Varying the support provided

The best support is hands-off, verbal instruction guiding the learner's actions, better still with an explanation as to why the action is required. This can be provided by adults or peers as long as they are well briefed.

Why teach this?

Whereas children have plenty of opportunities across the curriculum to present information with text and images, they are provided with far fewer opportunities to record and manipulate sounds. Linking writing to performance provides an incentive for ensuring that the quality of what is written is appropriate for an intended audience. The evaluation process is not only useful for focusing on the technical aspects of the production process; it helps the children re-examine the effectiveness of their work in relation to the work of others.

This project could be used in parallel with, or as a precursor or follow-up to, QCA ICT Unit 3B: *Manipulating sound*. The music compositions which children develop and produce in ICT Unit 3B could be used to accompany the action in their sound play – or at least be used as the introductory and concluding music. This project could be used as a precursor to ICT Unit 4A: *Writing for different audiences* or, with slight modification, could be used as a replacement. Some of the short focused tasks in Unit 4A could be modified to develop the skills and techniques needed for this project.

As children progress through their primary school less emphasis is placed on the development of speaking and listening and yet this is the principal means of communication in the world at large. Hearing yourself as others hear you is a valuable way of helping a child to appreciate the use of his or her voice. Sometimes the contexts for encouraging the children to write playscripts can be overly contrived and opportunities for performance are diminished owing to restrictions on time and organisational considerations. While some of the technicalities of performing a sound play are more demanding, the outcome is in a form which enables the children to focus on the quality of their own and others' performance and the effectiveness of the production.

It has been suggested that while children in primary classrooms often work in groups they seldom have the opportunity to work collaboratively on a single outcome (see Galton *et al.* 1999). The 'public' nature of the final product and the use of a computer for its composition provides ample opportunity for children to work in real collaboration. It has been shown, however, that children will not naturally work together unless they have been given clearly defined roles and guidance on what is expected of them (see Project 3, 'Why teach this?'). The roles taken by the children will be clearly defined for the performance, but they might need to be assigned specific (or shared) roles in the production process. For example, one child could be responsible for word processing (scribe), another for suggesting the dialogue (scriptwriter), a third for finalising the sound effects (effects manager) and another child could act as proof-reader.

The activities in this project relate to those in *Humanities* Project 8 (*Making an information source*), *Humanities* Project 9 (*A video of a visit to a place of worship*) and *Arts* Project 6 (*Sound pictures*) which address similar learning objectives in other subject contexts.

References and further reading

Brown, J., Collins, A. and DeGuid, P. (1989) 'Situated cognition and the culture of learning', *Educational Researcher*, 18, 32–42.

Galton, M., Hargreaves, L., Comber, C., Wall, D. and Pell, A. (1999) *Inside the Primary Classroom: 20 Years On*, London: Routledge and Kegan Paul.

Project Fact Card: Project 5: Villains

Who is it for?

- 7- to 8-year-olds (NC Levels 2–4)

What will the children do?

- Draw a picture of a villain using a paint package, online 'photofit' website or scan in a picture drawn by hand. They will then use this to produce a Wanted poster. Next, they will create a crime record card for their villain and enter the details into a prepared database. They will write a crime story for their villain and finally solve each other's crime stories using the search features of the database

What do I need to know?

- How to use a simple photofit picture creation tool or website OR how to create files of facial elements for a drawing program OR how to use a paint program OR a scanner
- The difference between paint and draw programs
- How to combine text and images in a word processor or desktop publishing software package
- How to create a database using a simple 'flat file' database program

What should the children know already?

- How to use a paint or draw program
- How to enter and format text in a word processor

What will the children learn?

- How to combine elements in a drawing program to create a finished image
- How to enter key facts into a database
- How to interrogate a database with simple and combined searches
- How to identify and communicate a description of a person
- How to write a crime story emulating a journalistic style

How to challenge the more able

- Using a greater range of picture elements
- Carrying out more complex searches
- Writing more sophisticated descriptions and crime stories

What resources will I need?

- A computer-based photofit creation program, access to an online photofit creation website, a drawing program with a library of facial features, a paint program, or a scanner
- A word processor or desktop publishing program
- One index card per child
- A simple 'flat file' database
- Newspaper stories of local crimes with partial descriptions of suspects
- An example crime story with a record card for the relevant villain

How to support the less able

- Using a simplified photofit and drawing package
- Using a writing frame and/or word bank for the Wanted poster and crime story
- Entering details into the database with more keywords and drop-down fields
- Providing more structured support when using the search tools

Why teach this?

- It addresses ICT NC KS2 PoS statements 1a, 1b, 1c, 2a, 3a, 3b
- It complements QCA ICT Scheme of Work Units 3A, 3C, (also 2E, 4A, 5B)
- It addresses English NC KS2 PoS statements En2, 2c, 2d, 3c, 5c, 5e, 9c; En3, 1a–f, 2a–f, 9a, 11
- It complements NLS units for Year 3 Term 3 Texts 12, 16, 17, 21, 22, 25

Villains

The activities described in this project have been written with 7- to 8-year-olds in mind, but with very little adaptation, the same tasks could be used with Year 3 or Year 5.

What will the children do?

Activity 1: Draw a photofit picture of their villain

Read an extract from a story featuring the description of a villain to the class (e.g. a Roald Dahl story such as *Fantastic Mr Fox* or *Matilda*). Show a photofit picture of the villain to the children and explain that they are going to produce a photofit of their own villain.

The image can be created in one of several ways (see 'What resources will I need?', below). The images are saved for use in the next activity.

In the plenary discussion ask why they selected particular features for their villains and the techniques which were used. Some children may have used some features in imaginative ways – for example, two eyebrows used to make a pencil-thin moustache.

Activity 2: Create a Wanted poster

Show a poster to the children and ask them what catches their attention the most. Emphasise the essential features – i.e. the eye-catching heading, the name of the villain, the picture and brief description. Pay particular attention to the presentation and phrasing of the description. An example Wanted poster is included on the CD-ROM which accompanies this book.

Ideally, the children should work individually as they will be producing their own individualised posters; however, it is likely that the children will work in pairs owing to the availability of resources. The children will need to import or insert the photofit picture they produced earlier.

You may decide to provide them with a template document and/or writing frame to guide the formatting and writing of the text. The emphasis should be on identifying the key distinguishing features which might not be evident from the picture (e.g. height, build) and maybe colouring of hair and eyes, particularly if the photofit pictures are black and white. The posters should be saved and printed out.

The concluding discussion should focus on those children who have produced particularly concise descriptions and those who have used expressive vocabulary. You could also focus on any children who have adopted an original approach to the presentation of their description (e.g. emboldening keywords or use of bulleted text).

Activity 3: Create a crime record card for their villain and enter the villain's details into a prepared database

Explain how a card index system works, preferably by demonstration. Discuss the essential features which they feel should be included on the record cards of their villains to allow a detective to identify them. The CD-ROM accompanying this book contains an example of a record card which you could print out and use to guide the children.

Distribute the cards on which the children enter the details for their villain. (NOTE: At this stage it is important that the children keep the identity and description of their villains to themselves to make the later solution of the crimes more realistic. Hence, the plenary should not be used to share the children's descriptions with each other.)

At this point you should slip a record card of your own villain into the pile of the children's villains and read the crime story which you have prepared or use the information and story provided (see 'What resources will I need?', below). Ask the children to suggest how they might use the cards to solve the crime. For example, if the crime was committed by someone with black hair and brown eyes, the cards showing black-haired villains should be extracted and then the brown-eyed villains drawn out from this subset. The third feature of the villain should then narrow the search down to one or two prime suspects.

Ask the children to collect crime stories from newspapers, particularly those which include descriptions of suspects, for the next activity.

Activity 4: Enter the details of their villain into the database

If your database does not allow multiple users (see 'What resources will I need?', below), you will either have to use one computer and have the children enter the details for their villain individually in turn, or enter the details of the villains yourself (or ask a teaching assistant or parent helper to do this).

Activity 5: Write a crime story for their villain

Read some (suitable) crime stories from the local newspaper, with an emphasis on:

- the structure of the story;

- how the first paragraph usually summarises the key events;

- how the middle section usually provides a description of the event and the suspect(s);

- how the final paragraph often provides details of who should be contacted;

- the vocabulary used in the story:

- the headline in particular;

- how the name and age of participants are usually included;

- keywords.

At this stage you might decide to reread the example crime story used in the previous activity to reinforce the structure and style of writing you are expecting. It is important that the children appreciate that they should include no more than three facts about their villain in the description otherwise the crime will be too easy to solve.

Ideally the children should write their own crime stories individually. You could split the class in two and have half creating their crime stories in the computer suite under the supervision of a teaching assistant while the rest are completing other work – and then swap them over.

Once all the stories have been entered and checked, they should be printed out ready for the next activity.

Activity 6: Solve other children's crime stories using the search features of a database

Demonstrate the search features of the database by solving your example crime story. Emphasise the parallels between the way the database searches through its records and the manual sorting of cards in Activity 3.

Printouts of the crime stories are distributed for the children to solve. They should complete a detective's report, identifying the villain they believe committed the crime and justifying the reasons for their choice(s).

Some crimes will result in more than one suspect. The children need to appreciate that this activity mirrors the real-life situation. The police sometimes cannot be certain who committed a crime and hence will question a series of suspects, gradually narrowing down the person they think is the most likely perpetrator.

You should also emphasise the relative ease with which the database enables them to narrow down their search compared with the card index system. You might want to discuss how companies hold information about their parents which is used for targeted mailings and telesales.

Review the project and remind them of the activities they have covered.

What should the children know already?

How to use a paint or draw program

It is not essential that the children are able to use a paint or draw program. For this project a draw program would be more useful than a paint program provided you have a file of picture elements (noses, hair styles, eyes, eyebrows, etc.) which the children can drag and drop into place on their portrait. This project would be a useful way of introducing the children to a draw program or discussing the different between paint and draw (see below).

How to enter and format text in a word processor

It is to be hoped the children's typing speed is sufficient for them to be able to produce a piece of work of reasonable length in the time available. The Wanted poster activity will provide you with an opportunity to assess the children's capabilities in using the keyboard and should enable you to decide whether writing frames and word banks might be needed to ensure the children are able to produce crime stories in the time you have available.

What resources will I need?

A computer-based photofit creation program, access to an online photofit creation website, a drawing program with a library of facial features, a paint program, or a scanner

There are a number of websites which can be used by children to produce photofit type pictures of faces:

- *Identikit* – www.whom.co.uk

- *Mugshot* – www.stuffucanuse.com

- *Face Maker* – www.freegames.ro

A search of the internet for 'face maker' or 'facemaker' will find a few more but these are the most appropriate for this project. Alternatively, *Facepaint2* (SEMERC) or some screens for *MyWorld* (Dial Solutions) (e.g. Clowns) can be used.

Another alternative is to use a library of Clip Art facial elements (eyes, noses, mouths, etc.) with a vector drawing program such as *Oak Draw* (Dial Solutions), *AspexDraw* (Aspex Software) or the drawing tools in *Microsoft Word* or *Talking First Word* (RM). A small sample of such elements is included on this book's CD-ROM.

A painting program (e.g. *Paint* (**Start > Programs > Accessories**), *Colour Magic* (RM), *Dazzle* (Indigo Learning)) could be used but the quality of the image which the children can produce in this way can prove frustrating.

If a scanner is available, the children could draw their villain using conventional materials and digitise the image. Alternatively, take a digital photo of each child and use the tools in an imaging program (e.g. *Photoshop Elements* (Adobe), *Photo Studio* (ArcSoft)) to touch up their own image.

A word processor or desktop publishing program

Any word processor will allow images to be inserted (e.g. *Word, Talking First Word, Granada Writer v3*). These can be used for both the Wanted poster and the crime stories activities. Desktop publishing packages (e.g. *Textease, Microsoft Publisher*) can also be used to create posters and crime stories.

One index card per child

These can be purchased from stationers, or you could make your own.

A simple 'flat file' database

Examples include *Information Workshop* (BlackCat), *Textease Database* (Softease), *Granada Database, Information Magic* (RM), *Junior Viewpoint* (Logotron). An interesting variation is *2Investigate* (2Simple) which emulates the physical sorting on screen by moving the cards into relevant piles or sets.

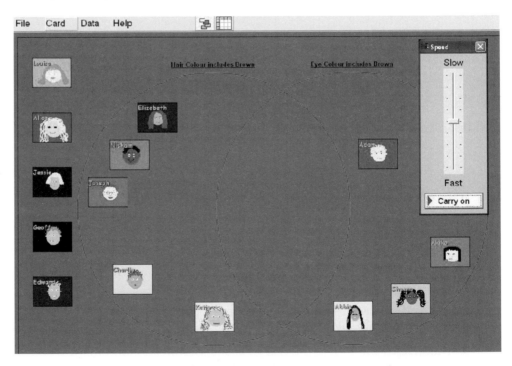

2Investigate *(2Simple) shows the children's cards being sorted into sets*

If your computers are networked, some databases (e.g. *2Investigate, Textease Database CT*) will automatically combine all the children's records into one database as they are entered on separate computers. If not, the children will have to take turns to enter their villain's details into the database on one computer, in which case you could use a laptop computer in the classroom. Alternatively, you (or a colleague) could transfer the information from the children's record cards on to the computer outside teaching hours.

Newspaper stories of local crimes with partial descriptions of suspects

In addition to an example crime story such as that reproduced here (written by a seven-year-old child) and provided in *Word* format on the CD-ROM accompanying this book, you should try to collect real crime stories extracted from local or national newspapers to help the children model their own stories (see the CD-ROM for examples).

Warrington Echo   *30th November 1822*

Stolen Goods

Soap and wine taken from canal boat

By Lisa, Our Crime Reporter

Mr and Mrs Black were on their canal boat last Friday night when it grew darker and a few drops of rain fell. Mr George Black, aged 39, and his wife, Sybil, 37, moored their boat, Princess, near to Preston Brook Warehouse and went to bed as the rain came down in sheets. Mrs Black went straight off to sleep after her tiring day but Mr Black lay there listening to the rain. Suddenly he felt the boat move. He grabbed his lantern and woke up his wife and climbed out of the door.

They saw a man loading six boxes of soap and two barrels of wine into a wagon. The man drove off in his wagon. Mr Black went to find his horse to give chase but, to his horror, he found their horse, Robin, had been taken too.

The Blacks were able to give a description of the man. He was average height, had black hair and wore black clothes. Mrs Black noticed he had a tattoo on one arm.

The canal company would be grateful for any information leading to the discovery of the missing goods and horse.

Robin

A crime story created with Talking First Word *(RM)*

An example crime story with a record card for the relevant villain

The headings and layout of the record card may differ from the example adjacent, depending on those which the children identify.

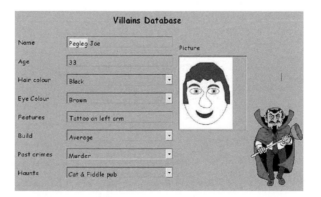

Example of a database record created with Textease Database

What do I need to know?

How to use a simple photofit picture creation tool or website OR how to create files of facial elements for a drawing program OR how to use a paint program or a scanner

The websites and programs for creating photofit pictures work in a similar way. You select face elements from a 'palette' and either drag and drop these on a face outline or click on the required element and reposition and rescale it by clicking buttons. The best way to gain confidence with these resources is to experiment with them. The children will probably find other tools and features which you have missed but this should be seen as an added bonus.

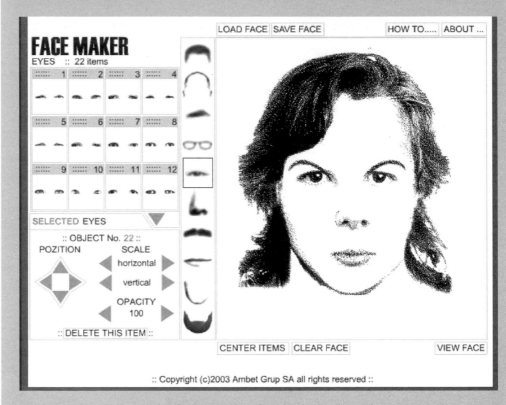

Example of a face produced on the Face Maker *website*

You will not be able to save the drawings from some websites. The image can be captured by pressing the **Print Screen** key on your keyboard (sometimes abbreviated to **Prt Scrn**). Open the *Paint* program (**Start > Programs > Accessories**) and click on **Paste** in the **Edit** menu. The whole screen will be pasted into *Paint*. Drag the selection tool around the face image and then click on **Copy** in the **Edit** menu. The face can then be pasted into your word processor.

If you are using a vector drawing program such as *MyWorld*, *Corel Draw* (Corel Corporation), *aspexDraw* or the drawing tools in *Word* or *Textease*, then you will need to find or create a library of face elements (eyes, noses, mouths, ears, etc.) for the children to drag, drop and resize. You could try drawing your own but this is very time consuming.

It is assumed you will know how to use a paint program and a scanner. Refer to 'What do I need to know?' in Project 2 for more guidance on using a scanner.

The difference between paint and draw programs

Vector drawing programs differ from paint programs in that each item created on the screen becomes a separate object which can be moved, resized, copied and pasted. In a paint program, once a shape has been drawn it becomes part of the background picture rather than an object floating above the background. The most commonly found drawing program in schools is *MyWorld*, which includes thousands of different background screens and libraries of objects which can be dragged and dropped. In addition to the flexibility which drawing programs have over paint programs, a great advantage is that drawings take up far less of the computer's memory than paintings.

The drawing tools in *MS Word* are another resource which could be used to gain familiarity with the tools and techniques needed.

To use the drawing tools in *MS Word*

Create a new document in *MS Word* (by selecting **New** from the **File** menu). Show the **Drawing** toolbar by selecting **View > Toolbars > Drawing**:

The **Drawing** toolbar can be dragged into position on the top, bottom or edges of the *Word* window. Clicking on the relevant tools and dragging on the screen to resize and reshape them will enable you to create drawings from a series of elements or 'objects'. The face below uses a series of ovals for the basic shape and the eyes, moon shapes for the mouth and eyebrows, a 'scribble' shape for the

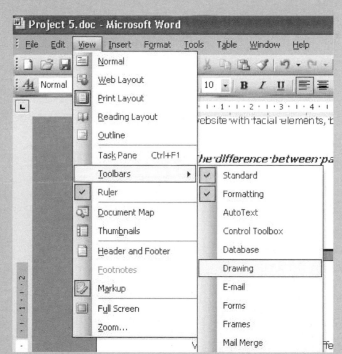

nose and a 'freehand' shape for the hair which are all found in the **AutoShapes** menu. The drawing tools in other word processors (e.g. *Textease*, *Granada Writer v3*) and drawing programs work in a similar way.

> ### How to combine text and images in a word processor or desktop publishing software package
>
> Inserting images into word-processed documents is now a very straightforward business. With educational word processors such as *Textease*, images are inserted by dragging and dropping from a drop-down window. Word processors such as *Word* use the **Insert** menu.
>
> ### How to create a database using a simple 'flat file' database program
>
> The process for setting up a database is fundamentally the same regardless of the database you are using:
>
> - Create a new database.
> - Define the fields needed for the children to enter the details about their villains (e.g. name, age, hair colour, eye colour, etc.).
> - Design the way the records will appear on the screen (e.g. the position of each field, the headings, the background colour and add some Clip Art).
> - Enter details for a villain of your own (or use the example above).
> - Save the file and load onto each of the computers to be used by the children.
>
> An example database file is provided on the CD-ROM that comes with this book in various formats (text (tsv, csv), *Textease*). For more information on creating database files, see *Maths Project 6 – Statistical Investigations 1*.

What will the children learn?

How to combine elements in a drawing program to create a finished image

If a drawing program is used, this activity could contribute to the children's understanding of how these can be used to create original images.

How to enter key facts into a database

The children need to appreciate the importance of entering the information accurately, without spelling mistakes. If, for example, a child spells 'tattoo' as 'tatoo', then a search for villains with a 'tattoo' will not find the misspelt entry.

How to interrogate a database with simple and combined searches

Most of the databases listed above allow for complex searches (using 'and' or 'or'). Initially, it is advisable for the children to learn how to search for records which satisfy one criterion (e.g. hair colour) and then narrow the search by searching these records for the next criterion (e.g. eye colour). If necessary, the children might need to carry out a third search on these records (e.g. for tattoo). The advantage of using a progressive search is that it mirrors the physical action of sorting the record cards into piles as in Activity 3. With a combined search (e.g. hair colour = black AND eye colour = brown AND features includes tattoo) there is a greater risk the search will reveal no suitable matches, particularly if the description has been mistyped.

How to identify and communicate a description of a person

Extracting the key features from a crime story requires the development of key skills such as skimming and scanning, identifying keywords and extracting meaning. Similarly, creating a description requires the children to consider and communicate the key features of their own villain.

How to write a crime story emulating a journalistic style

Children will rarely get this right in their first draft. You will need to make a professional judgement on whether you correct the children's drafts by marking, whether you use peers or buddies, whether you encourage the children to self-correct, or whether you are prepared to allow an approximation to the style. The example crime story shown above was achieved by a combination of self-correction and discussion with the teacher, comparing an example story produced by the teacher with the child's.

Challenging the more able and supporting the less able: modifying the project for older and younger pupils

Adjusting the complexity of the drawing activity

MyWorld screens and libraries are not only easier for the children to use; the software will probably already be familiar to them. Some 'face maker' websites are easier to use as they require less decision making by the children. Increasing the number of choices available to the children will increase the level of challenge.

Adjusting the complexity of the searches

Children with limited experience of using computers will need to have the search tools explained more carefully and maybe have the searching task (Activity 6) scaffolded into a series of sub-tasks. As indicated above, a series of simple searches is conceptually more straightforward than a combined search using Boolean terms (AND, OR, NOT). Some children will quickly realise that time can be saved by conducting a combined search and, provided they realise how the search is working, they can be encouraged.

Adjusting the level of challenge in writing the descriptions and crime stories

Some children will benefit from a whole-class brainstorming session on descriptive words and phrases which are then turned into a word bank to provide those children who lack ideas and/or have a limited vocabulary with starting points. If you have an interactive whiteboard, the bank can be created instantaneously and saved to the network for the children to access.

Making suggestions (e.g. through shared writing) as to how a draft story can be developed can help a child appreciate how a simplistic response to the task can be developed into a work of literary merit.

Matching the way the data are entered to the needs of the children

If the database is created using keywords or drop-down fields from which the children select appropriate words, then this will not only save typing but will ensure the words are spelled correctly.

Why teach this?

This project not only provides the children with an opportunity to develop data-handling skills; it sets the activities into an interesting and imaginative context which should make it more memorable. The creation of the portrait, the poster production and the writing of the crime story provide ample opportunities for the children to develop the skills and knowledge needed to consider the needs of their audience – particularly as they know the reader will need to use the information to try and solve the crime.

This project could be used as a direct replacement for both QCA ICT Units 3A: *Combining text and graphics* and 3C: *Introduction to databases* or could be used as a preliminary or replacement for some aspects of Unit 4A: *Writing for different audiences* (writing a newspaper report). Some of the focused tasks in Units 3A and 3C could be adapted and used in this project, particularly if the children are lacking in confidence or experience with the basic skills of word processing and image manipulation.

Rather than attempting to address all the relevant areas of learning in literacy, narrow the focus to specific aspects most relevant for the children's needs. For example, if you feel the children need more experience of descriptive writing, the focus could be shifted to vocabulary extension activities. If, however, you feel the greatest need is for the children to summarise and extract key information from texts, then greater emphasis could be put into the development of this aspect of the project work. The motivation for this will depend on the timing for the delivery of this project. For example, those following the literacy framework as presented in the documentation will probably find this project is more relevant in Term 3 of Year 3.

The specific areas of language learning which this project work can be used to address are:

⊙ descriptive writing and vocabulary extension work;

⊙ opportunities for drafting and redrafting written work to emulate a particular genre (i.e. newspaper reporting);

⊙ the reinforcement of information text handling skills such as skimming, scanning and the identification of key facts;

⊙ concise writing and elaboration/extemporisation;

⊙ refining and extending skills needed for efficient information searching.

See also *Humanities* Project 6 (*Using a database to analyse census data*) and *Maths* Project 6 (*Statistical investigations 1*) for related activities.

Project Fact Card: Project 6: Imaginative e-mail

Who is it for?

- 7- to 8-year-olds (NC Levels 2–4)

What will the children do?

- After responding to e-mails from a character in a story they will communicate with children in another class over collaborative writing. They will go on to improve a 'skeleton' story and write a review for a story produced by children in a parallel class. Finally, they will respond to a review of their own story

What should the children know already?

- How to enter text using a keyboard

What do I need to know?

How to use the school's e-mailing system
- How to manage the children's e-mail accounts
- The school's (and/or LA's) policy for safe use of e-mail
- How to receive and send e-mails and attachments using an e-mail program

What resources will I need?

- An e-mail address for the lead character in a story
- E-mail accounts for the children and a safe/secure e-mailing client
- A colleague teaching a parallel class (in the same school or another school – could be in another country)
- (Optional) An adult willing and able to participate in a role-playing situation
- A story/picture book with a key main character suitable for stimulating discussion and questioning

What will the children learn?

- Safe use of e-mail
- How to write and respond to e-mails
- How to add and open attachments to e-mails
- How to condense information and communicate efficiently in writing
- How to develop a skeleton text into a more detailed and elaborated story
- Making decisions and taking account of others' views through 'Exploratory Talk'

How to challenge the more able

- Using more complex scenarios
- Contributing to an online story
- Corresponding with an ePal

How to support the less able

- Pairing with more experienced but well-briefed peers
- Providing adult support

Why teach this?

- It addresses ICT NC KS2 PoS statements 1a, 1c, 3a, 3b
- It complements QCA ICT Scheme of Work Unit 3E (and 4A)
- It addresses English NC KS2 PoS statements En1, 3a–e, 4a, 11a; En2, 2a, 2b; En3, 1c, 1d, 2f, 9a, 9b, 9d, 11, 12
- It complements NLS units for Year 3 Term 3 Texts 1, 2, 5, 10, 11, 13, 14, 20, 21

Imaginative e-mail

Although this project is designed for 7- to 8-year-olds, it could be adapted for any age group by adjusting the level of support provided or increasing the level of linguistic challenge through the use of the initial story.

What will the children do?

Activity 1: Write e-mails to a character in a story

Well before you intend to teach the project, set up an e-mail account (e.g. through Hotmail) for a key character in the story you will be using. If you would like the responses to the children's e-mails to be immediate, a colleague (or partner) needs to be briefed about the character and the story and be available on another computer when this first activity is being taught.

Use a story which will appeal to the children's interests and read an extract which is sufficient to stimulate their interest and curiosity in the main character.

If the children are unfamiliar with the rules for 'Exploratory Talk', these should be discussed at this point (see Project 3, 'Why teach this?') to ensure that the next part of the activity is productive.

Once the scene has been set, the children are organised into smaller groups to produce three questions they would like to ask the character. For example, if using the *Ffangs* story (see 'What resources will I need?', below), one question could be about his reasons for wanting to become human, another about how he is going to try to become human and a third asking for his response to a suggestion they have for helping him. It is important that the children are reminded about reaching decisions through Exploratory Talk. One child should act as scribe for each group to record their questions.

The groups identify their favourite question which you send as an e-mail to Ffangs. If a colleague is on hand to respond, the return e-mails can be read aloud and/or presented to the children via an interactive whiteboard or projector. Otherwise this discussion will have to be postponed until the following day to allow you time to respond on behalf of the character.

At the conclusion of the activity you could ask the children to speculate on the rest of the story and, if time permits, read the rest of the story to them.

Activity 2: Communicate with children in another class over collaborative writing

Before the lesson, explain the activity to a colleague in a parallel class and synchronise the timing of the lessons. The children's e-mail accounts will need setting up and checking.

Explain the activity to the children and demonstrate by corresponding with your colleague, taking turns to write sentences in a story with the children's help. For example, you may decide to start with the sentence *'Once upon a time a chicken and a duck went for a walk in the country'*. This is sent off as an e-mail and your colleague sends the next sentence, e.g. *'They were just about to walk across the old wooden bridge over the stream when a wolf appeared on the other side'*. Ask the children to suggest the next sentence – quickly so as not to keep the other children and teacher waiting.

Each group is allocated an e-mail address for its own and its corresponding parallel group and the children are despatched to their computers. Preliminary introductory e-mails are exchanged in which the children explain who they are and decide which group will write the first sentence. 'Exploratory Talk' rules are enforced with the children taking turns to be typist. Once the sentence has been despatched (remembering that time is of the essence), the children await the reply – they should, however, be discussing how the story might progress. Once the reply has been received they must quickly decide on the most appropriate response and send it.

Towards the end of the lesson, the final e-mail, containing the story so far, will need to be printed out. Each group reads out its story and then evaluate the lesson by asking the children to decide:

⊙ What they like most about each story

⊙ Which story they think is the most coherent

⊙ How they might improve that story

Activity 3: Improve the 'skeleton' stories

Show the children the example 'story' which you and your colleague started in the previous activity. Ask the children to suggest ways in which the first two sentences might be improved. The children can add or change words or suggest a new intervening sentence. Continue with pairs of sentences until you feel the children have understood the task.

In their original groups the children retrieve their final e-mail and copy and paste their skeleton story into a word processor. If the children lack the confidence or technical skills to do this, you could prepare the word processor files for them.

Tell them they will be sending their improved version of the story to the group in the parallel class who will mark it and comment on its quality. They will be marking and sending back the story which the parallel group will be writing.

The children work collaboratively to improve the coherence and quality of their 'skeleton story'. This may take more than one lesson, depending on the time available and the capabilities of the children.

When the stories have been completed they are sent as attachments via e-mail to their parallel group. It is advisable to check the stories before allowing them to be sent off. When they receive the parallel group's version of their joint story they should print it out ready for the next activity.

Activity 4: Write a review of a shared story

Liaise with your colleague in the parallel class to ensure that all the stories have been completed and dispatched. This may take several lessons depending on timetables and the complexity of the stories. It is a good idea to check the e-mail accounts to ensure all groups have received an e-mail with an attached story which will open successfully.

With the class, discuss the criteria they will use to assess the stories and agree on the way feedback will be provided (e.g. they must identify and praise what they feel are good ideas; any criticism must be constructive; only three mistakes are allowed to be corrected; etc.). These criteria should be agreed by the whole class and made into either a poster or a handout.

Remind the children about the purpose of the activity and the rules of Exploratory Talk. Explain the format for the review and if a template or writing frame is used, show the children how to access it. Demonstrate how to open an e-mail attachment.

The groups open the e-mails from their parallel groups and read the attached stories (printing out copies for each member of the group if necessary). Working collaboratively, they write a review of the story which is printed out.

In the plenary session, each group reads aloud the story from its parallel group (or an extract if they are too long) and then its review. The other children are invited to comment or make suggestions.

You should edit the reviews before they are dispatched – or 'mark' them making suggested revisions. The reviews could be sent by the teacher or by the children (depending on timetabling for the computer suite or availability of an internet-connected classroom computer).

Activity 5: Respond to a review of their story

Remind the children about the previous activity and explain the purpose and structure of this activity.

In groups, the review of their story is opened and the children discuss their response. For example, they may decide to change part of their story or to explain why an event happened in a particular way.

In a plenary session, the groups take turns to read out the review of their story and their response. The other children comment about the appropriateness of the group's response and, if necessary, suggest amendments.

The groups return to the computer and, if necessary, make amendments before dispatching their response to the review.

What should the children know already?

How to enter text using a keyboard

You could use the same typist for each task for speed and accuracy or rotate the role with each activity to ensure all the children gain hands-on experience of using the e-mail program. There are no additional computer skills needed in composing and sending e-mails.

What resources will I need?

An e-mail address for the lead character in a story

The easiest way to set up an e-mail account for your character is on the Hotmail website (www.hotmail.com). There are several other free webmail providers which you could access: you might decide to set up an e-mail address with your own home Internet Service Provider (ISP), or you could set one up through the school's e-mail client (though this is likely to have an unimaginative name and an address similar to the children's which might affect their involvement in the task).

E-mail accounts for the children and a safe/secure e-mailing client

If you are uncertain about how this is achieved in your school, you should consult the ICT co-ordinator. All schools should have access to safe, well-monitored e-mail systems provided through the Local Authority (LA). It is important that the LA and school guidance and procedures are followed (see 'What do I need to know?', below).

A colleague teaching a parallel class (in the same school or another school – could be in another country)

The easiest way to set this up is through personal contact. If you want to be more adventurous and explore the possibility of setting up the project with a teacher in another locality or country, you could use one of the following:

- www.epals.com
- www.gigglepotz.com
- www.europeanschoolsnet.org

(Optional) An adult willing and able to participate in a role-playing situation

If you would like responses to the children's e-mails in Activity 1 to be immediate, you need to ensure you have a willing and well-briefed colleague poised over an internet-connected computer while the lesson is being taught.

A story/picture book with a key main character suitable for stimulating discussion and questioning

The story used as an example in this project is taken from *Ffangs the Vampire Bat and the Kiss of Truth* by Ted Hughes (Faber & Faber, 1986). The key to choosing a story (or chapter) for this project is to find one in which there is a key character involved in an interesting plot.

What do I need to know?

How to use the school's e-mailing system

How to manage the children's e-mail accounts

The school's (and/or LA's) policy for safe use of e-mail

Although e-mailing systems work in similar ways the precise procedures for creating e-mail accounts for the children and ensuring the e-mail program is set up to communicate with the internet will vary according to the system used by the school and the LA. The school's ICT co-ordinator should know how to set up the system or who to contact to ensure the system is functioning correctly.

Similarly, all schools should have a policy for making use of the internet safe, particularly e-mail. The policy may require you to send a letter to parents explaining the project, reassuring them of the safeguards the school has in place and seeking their permission for their child to participate in the project. If in doubt, refer to the guidance provided on the *DfES Superhighway Safety* website: www.safety.ngfl.gov.uk

For further ideas and case studies using e-mail in the primary classroom, see: www.rm.com

How to receive and send e-mails and attachments using an e-mail program

E-mail programs vary slightly in the way information is presented on the screen but they all perform the same function. Each will include an inbox showing e-mails which have been received, and they will all have a button or menu item allowing the user to create a new e-mail message. They all have an address book which stores names and e-mail addresses and all will include some means of adding and opening attachments.

An attachment is a file or document, such as a saved word processor document or a saved picture, which can be added to an e-mail message. When the attachment is received it can be opened by the recipient using the relevant program (e.g. *MS Word*, *Textease*, an image-handling program, etc.). In *Outlook* (Microsoft), documents are attached by clicking on a button on the toolbar shown when creating a new message:

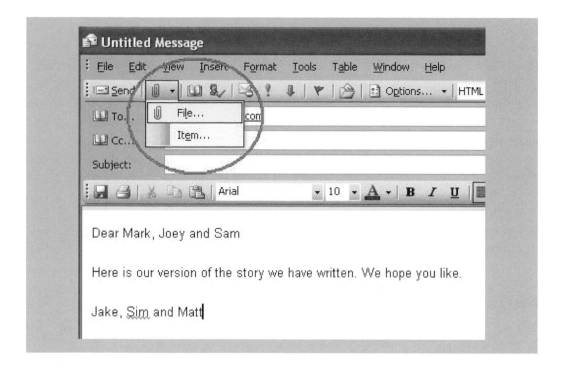

What will the children learn?

Safe use of e-mail

Many children will have access to the internet at home so it is very important you make them aware of the dangers of sending and receiving e-mails to/from people they do not know. The key principles for safe e-mail use are:

⊙ Always inform an adult when you are using e-mail

⊙ Never reveal your password to anyone – not even to your best friend

⊙ Do not reveal any personal information about yourself

⊙ Do not open an e-mail or an attachment unless you are certain what it is and who it is from

⊙ If you receive an e-mail which worries or upsets you, tell an adult

⊙ Remember that people can pretend to be someone else when they are using e-mail

How to write and respond to e-mails

Just as there are protocols and etiquette associated with writing letters, there are guiding principles to writing e-mails. Concise writing is essential. Some of the conventions associated with considerate use of e-mail include:

⊙ Do not write in capitals – this is equivalent to shouting

⊙ Explain yourself clearly and simply

- Never be rude or unpleasant – all e-mails are monitored

- Do not hit the 'send' button until you have read your message twice

- Do not send attachments larger than 1 Mb (= 1000 Kb)

How to add and open attachments to e-mails

As indicated above, with most e-mail programs this is achieved by simply clicking on a button. The children will also need to know how to locate where the document has been saved and how to save a document in a place where they will later be able to find it. This involves making use of the **Open . . .** and **Save As . . .** dialogue boxes, which are broadly similar for all programs.

How to condense information and communicate efficiently in writing

You could use this project to reinforce, apply or introduce the children to efficient note-taking techniques. E-mails tend to be written in concise form, without elaboration – incomplete sentences and phrases are permitted provided the meaning is clear. Similarly, words can be abbreviated as reqd.

How to develop a skeleton text into a more detailed and elaborated story

The added incentive of sending their story to a similar group of children will encourage the children to think very carefully about the needs of their audience and the way the story is developed. This activity could become a key focus for the project and be covered in several consecutive lessons, as you focus on developing different aspects of the story such as improving description of characters and settings or adding tension through the use of key phrases and plot structures.

Making decisions and taking account of others' views through 'Exploratory Talk'

Central to the success of this project is the relationships between group members. It has been shown that children who are taught how to reach collaborative decisions by engaging in Exploratory Talk take more account of each other's views and are more considerate in their dealings with their classmates (see 'Why teach this?', below, and Project 3). Setting the climate for Exploratory Talk through establishing and conforming to agreed rules is an essential initial stage of this process.

Challenging the more able and supporting the less able: modifying the project for older and younger pupils

Adjusting the content and focus of the story

The choice of the initial story will clearly have a bearing on the levels of engagement and the responses of the children. The *Ffangs* story used above is quite challenging in terms of its literary form and content but extracts from simpler or more challenging children's novels or epic poetry could be used to match the capabilities of the children.

Contributing to an online story

As a follow-up or for groups which complete their stories before the others, you could suggest they contribute an episode to an online story such as *The Neverending Tale* (www.coder.com/creations/tale/) or get the computer to write them a *Wacky Web Tale* (www.eduplace.com/tales/).

Corresponding with an ePal

If you have established contact with a colleague through the ePal website or similar, you could consider extending the project by encouraging the children to correspond via e-mail with a partner in the parallel class.

Pairing less experienced children with more experienced but well-briefed peers

The make-up of the groups is very important for the success of the project. Exploratory Talk will not be achieved if there is an overbearing, dominant child who is not willing (or able) to consider the views of others. Similarly, a more experienced or confident child could dominate a group if the others feel insecure. However, less experienced children can benefit from working alongside more capable peers provided the climate is right and the more experienced children are clearly briefed about their responsibilities in supporting and involving the others. Matching the groups in the parallel class should also ensure that the quality of the responses are comparable.

In some schools, children from an older class are allocated to support groups in the computer suite with technical and/or learning guidance.

Adult support

If some children are very inexperienced with using computers, then it might be necessary to draft additional adult support to work alongside the groups. The adults will need to be well briefed on the type and level of support they are expected to provide to ensure that learning opportunities are not missed.

Why teach this?

In addition to the skills of sending and receiving e-mails and attachments, copying and pasting between applications and making use of the editing tools in a word processor, the children will have to consider the relevance of the information they send to recipients to ensure it is accessible and clear. In addition, they will have to take account of the interests of their intended (unseen) audience in the parallel class. They will need to consider the impact of layout and format (e.g. italicising, emboldening, the use of indents, etc.) on the readability of the completed story as well as the choice of words. The reviewing process should help them consider not only the parallel group's use of presentation techniques but also their own.

This project is a direct replacement for QCA ICT Unit 3E: *E-mail*, covering most of the learning objectives (apart from the use of address books). It also addresses many of the learning outcomes for QCA Unit 4A: *Writing for different audiences* through the use of story writing rather than recounts. Some of the focused tasks from Unit 4A could be incorporated with the activities in this project if a more structured approach to learning about the use of editing tools is required.

The collaborative nature of all the group-based activities and the emphasis on Exploratory Talk makes this project particularly valuable for developing important aspects of the children's speaking and listening skills. Discussing the responses to e-mails and working together on the content and structure of the shared story writing provide motivating and meaningful contexts for reaching joint decisions. There is a heavy emphasis on writing for different purposes in this project – posing questions, the shared writing of a story, enhancing a skeleton story, writing a review. Rather than attempting to address all aspects in equal depth it is suggested that one or two are selected as a key focus and that more time and teaching input is devoted to these.

For related activities, see *Humanities* Project 7 (*Link with a contrasting locality*) which focuses on online communication using blogging and/or a photo-sharing website.

Project Fact Card: Project 7: Photo-dramas

Who is it for?

- 8- to 9-year-olds (NC Levels 2–5)

What will the children do?

- The children will use digital stills cameras to record their dramatisation of a story as an animated photo-presentation. The children will either identify an issue relevant to their own lives or select a short story. They will then work in groups to create a storyboard for a photo-drama. After enacting the drama and taking digital photos of the scenes, they will organise and edit their digital pictures. Using a slideshow program they will create a presentation depicting the drama incorporating digital effects and a soundtrack. Finally, they will evaluate their own and each other's presentations

What should the children know already?

- How to enter text with a keyboard

What will the children learn?

- How to storyboard a photo-drama
- How to use a digital camera
- The importance of viewpoint
- Basic digital photo editing
- How to create a linear presentation
- How to evaluate a photo-drama

What do I need to know?

- How to take digital pictures and transfer them to a computer
- How to create a presentation
- (Optional) How to add callout speech bubbles to an image in a presentation

What resources will I need?

- One or more digital stills camera(s)
- A computer with the relevant software installed for uploading pictures from a digital camera
- A photo-editing software package
- A presentation software package

How to challenge the more able

- More complex storylines
- Create their own music to accompany the photo-drama

How to support the less able

- Provide the children with a storyline to dramatise or adapt
- Create a template for the children's presentation
- More support (adult or peer)

Why teach this?

- It addresses ICT NC KS2 PoS statements 2a, 3a, 3b
- It complements QCA ICT Scheme of Work Unit 4A (also 6A)
- It addresses English NC KS2 PoS statements En1, 3a, 3b, 4b, 10a–c, 11a–c; En2, 4e; En3, 2a–f
- It complements NLS units for Year 4 Term 1 Text 1, 4, 5, 6, 9, 13; Year 4 Term 2 Text 12; Year 4 Term 3 Texts 1, 11 (also Year 5 Term 1 Sentence 5, Texts 5, 20)
- It develops aspects of children's visual literacy
- It shows what information can be communicated through a picture
- It teaches children how to use viewpoint to communicate an impression

Photo-dramas

This project has been written with 8- to 9-year-old children in mind as a means of recording drama and could be used as a preparatory activity for exploring direct speech which is scheduled by the National Literacy Framework for the first term of Year 5. The level of ICT challenge could be enhanced through increasing the complexity of the presentation or the sophistication of the storyline.

What will the children do?

The activities described below are group based – each group producing its own photo-drama. As an introduction or as an alternative, the whole class could work on a single whole-class photo-drama. This organisation puts the teacher more in control and will require fewer resources. Sufficient photos could be taken to allow pairs of children to work on the editing of each picture. However, this organisational approach provides fewer opportunities for the children to develop their ICT capabilities.

Activity 1: Create a simple photo-drama presentation and evaluate its effectiveness

Create a simple (e.g. three picture) live photo-drama with some volunteer children. For example, the story could feature a classroom incident such as a child getting another into trouble for talking. If you are using *PhotoStory3* (Microsoft), add a simple voice-over dialogue to the presentation and (maybe) musical accompaniment. If *PowerPoint* is used, add some speech-bubble dialogue.

   NOTE: Take five pictures of each scene, three from a normal eye-level viewpoint (wide view, mid-view, close-up), one from a low viewpoint and one from a high viewpoint. When composing the story, ask the children to choose the viewpoint which they feel tells that part of the story the best. The children may not, at this stage, appreciate that there are subtle differences in the way the viewpoint affects the portrayal of the scene – that is, a lower viewpoint makes a character look dominant, a close-up can increase empathy, etc. But when they come to take their own pictures they will begin to think about differences in the way the image can be presented.

Discuss the story and its presentation and identify the differences between it and a conventional story. For example:

Advantages	Disadvantages
● More interesting ● Good for non-readers ● Realistic ● Good for 'real-life' stories ● A novelty	● Cannot be read in bed ● Cannot be used for fantasy stories ● Could become boring after a while (a film is better)

Produce a set of criteria which can be used for evaluation. For example:

⊙ The story is appropriate for a photo-story	Very	Some	Not
⊙ The pictures are well organised	Very	Some	Not
⊙ The pictures are clear	Very	Some	Not
⊙ The dialogue tells the story well	Very	Some	Not
⊙ The story is interesting	Very	Some	Not
⊙ The story is realistic	Very	Some	Not

The criteria are noted down for use in Activities 5 and 6.

Activity 2: Identify an issue relevant to their own lives and create a storyboard for a photo-drama or select a short story for photo-dramatisation

If you feel the children are able to identify their own scenarios based, for example, on incidents in their own lives, then the introduction to this activity could be fairly brief and the children allocated to groups. If, on the other hand, you feel the children need more support in identifying a suitable plot for their own dramas, you could present them with a situation such as a new child joining the class or playground bullying. This could be presented as a skeleton story (see example below). Alternatively, you could read or give them a conventional short story and ask them to dramatise it.

> ## Skeleton story
>
> 1. 3 girls skipping in the playground
> 2. Boy starts spoiling the game
> 3. One girl goes to tell the teacher on duty

> 4. Boy is told off and sent inside
> 5. Classroom – boy tells girl he is going to 'get her' after school
> 6. Girl tells her friends
> 7. After school – boy waits for girl by gates
> 8. Girl appears with friends
> 9. Boy too scared to 'get her'
> 10. Girls happy to be friends and stick together
> 11. Boy unhappy – has no friends

The children need to be shown how to create a simple storyboard. In the example shown opposite, the children have used a storyboard to decide how the playground bullying incident can be presented as a series of images.

Working in groups of 4–5, the children plot their photo-dramas using a blank storyboard. The group discussion could be linked to a practical drama lesson in which the scene is acted out. At this stage, writing dialogue is not essential. A template for a storyboard in *Word* format is provided on the CD-ROM accompanying this book.

NOTE: School-based stories are preferable unless you intend to coincide the photographing of the dramas with a class trip.

The groups explain how they intend to dramatise their stories.

Activity 3: Enact the photo-drama

The organisation for this activity will be dependent on the number of cameras and the availability of computers for downloading the images. If you have several cameras and access to a computer suite in which all computers have the software needed for downloading the images, then this activity could be taught as a single lesson.

If there is only one digital camera and the classroom computer is used for downloading the images, then this activity will have to be spread over a series of lessons, with different groups using the equipment in turn.

If one camera is used, it may have sufficient memory for several stories to be photographed before they need to be downloaded. You could do this yourself at the end of the day.

The procedures for using the camera and downloading the images to the computer(s) are demonstrated and the children briefed on the activity (and your expectations for their behaviour).

The children work together taking the photos they need for their dramas.

Activity 4: Organise and edit the images

The photos will need to be checked and organised into folders (either on the school's network or on CD) for the groups to use. It is advisable to make a back-up CD of the images in case the images accidentally become corrupted or deleted.

Demonstrate the editing features of a simple photo-editing package (e.g. *Microsoft photo editor*). The children may need to crop or rotate the photos they have created. Alternatively, they might want to add some effects to enhance the

Title: The Bully

Name(s): Sally Tina Rose Julie

1.	2.
3 girls skipping in the playground	Boy starts spoiling the game
3.	4.
One girl goes to tell the teacher on duty	Boy is told off and sent inside
5.	6.
Classroom – boy tells girl he is going to 'get her' after school	Girl tells her friends

dramatic impact of the image (e.g. colour tinting or reducing to black and white). You should also show them how and where to open and save their images.

The children work in their groups, checking their photos and editing as necessary, and identify the photos which they think are the most effective in telling their story.

Each group presents to the rest of the class the image which it feels is the most effective, justifying this choice in terms of the story and the message the image portrays. The images could either be presented using an interactive whiteboard or printed out.

Activity 5: Create a presentation depicting the drama

It is advisable to check the images the children will be using to ensure they have been saved appropriately. You might need to reduce the size of some images if they are consuming a lot of memory.

Demonstrate the presentation, showing the basic features:

⊙ how new slides are created;

⊙ how images are inserted.

Remind the children about the evaluation criteria they identified in the first activity and use these to guide the production of their own story. Brief them on the way in which the opinions of all members of the group should be taken into account using the rules for Exploratory Talk (see Project 3, 'Why teach this?').

The children work in groups to create their photo-dramas. Once they have created a few slides they could then be shown some of the more advanced presentation effects. For example:

⊙ How transitions and zoom effects are added (*PhotoStory*)

⊙ How a commentary is added (*PhotoStory*)

⊙ How speech-bubble 'callouts' are added to a slide (*PowerPoint*)

Check on progress and discuss any general technical issues which may have arisen. Highlight one or two groups' work which you feel exemplifies the sort of response you are seeking.

NOTE: This activity may take one or two lessons to complete.

Activity 6: Evaluate their own and each other's dramas

Select one group's presentation as the basis for the plenary task. The children need to apply the criteria which were identified in the first activity. The choice for each criterion must be justified with a positive or constructive comment.

The children work in pairs to evaluate one or two presentations (depending on time), completing an evaluation sheet using the agreed criteria.

Any presentations which were felt to be particularly effective (e.g. scoring 'Very' on all criteria) are shown and discussed.

What should the children know already?

How to enter text with a keyboard

There is not a great deal of typing needed for this project, but familiarity with the keyboard will help to speed up the process.

All other skills and knowledge needed are taught through the project.

What resources will I need?

One or more digital stills camera(s)

Most schools have at least one digital stills camera of reasonable quality; however, for this activity, inexpensive digital cameras could be used – which can be purchased for less than £30.

A computer with the relevant software installed for uploading pictures from a digital camera

Digital cameras are usually accompanied by a disc containing the software needed for transferring the pictures from the camera to the computer. The software tends to be specific to the make and sometimes even the model of camera being used. If, for some reason, the disc is not available, the website for the company who manufactured the camera will probably include a section where the 'driver' software for your camera can be downloaded (often found under the 'technical' or 'support' heading). Make sure you download the software which is specific to the model of camera you have – check the model name/number on the camera.

A photo-editing software package

Most digital cameras include photo-editing software on the installation disc which comes with them. However, the licence will probably only allow you to install the software on one computer. The more recent versions of Microsoft Office include a basic photo-editing program, which will perform the basic functions needed for this task:

⊙ Cropping – being able to trim the image to cut out unnecessary background clutter

⊙ Brightness and contrast adjustments – useful if an image is too dark to be seen

⊙ Colour controls – to change an image into black and white

⊙ Digital effects – for example, making it look foggy, or changing an image to make it look like a watercolour painting

Alternatively, you can download free photo-editing programs from the internet. The two most well known are:

⊙ *The Gimp* – available from www.gimp.org

⊙ *VCW VicMan* photo editor – available from www.vicman.net

The *Paint* program which comes with all PCs provides very basic editing features. It can be found by clicking on **Start > Programs > Accessories**. Images can be cropped by using the selection tool, then copying and pasting into a new picture.

The rectangular select tool is dragged over the area of the picture required. This is copied and pasted into a new picture.

A presentation software package

Presentation packages enable the user to create a series of slides which are presented on screen in sequence. *PowerPoint* (part of *Microsoft Office*) allows considerable control over the way in which the slides are presented and for the purposes of this project allows the user to insert speech bubbles (callouts). Other presentation packages include *Textease Presenter* and *Granada Internet Odyssey.*

PhotoStory3 runs only on Windows XP and can be downloaded free of charge from: www.microsoft.com

NOTE: *PhotoStory3* includes basic photo-editing features.

What do I need to know?

How to take digital pictures and transfer them to a computer

In most cases, all that needs to be done is to switch on the camera and the computer and then link them via the cable which is provided. The computer should then detect the camera and run a program which asks you whether you want to save, print or e-mail the pictures. Saving the pictures will usually transfer them to the **My Pictures** folder in **My Documents**. If in doubt, consult the manual which accompanied the camera.

Using a card reader

If your computer has a card reader, or a card reader is connected to your computer, the memory card which the camera uses to store its pictures can be removed from the camera and inserted into the relevant slot. If this action does not trigger the running of the transfer program, the memory card can usually be found by double clicking on **My Computer** (on the desktop). Open the card (often labelled **Removable disk**) by double clicking on it. This should show you a folder in which are stored all the pictures on the disc. These can be dragged and dropped from this folder to another folder such as **My Pictures** in **My Documents**.

How to create a presentation

Creating a presentation using a presentation program such as *PowerPoint*

The process for creating a slide show with *Powerpoint* involves these steps:

- Open the program
- Choose a design for your slide show
- Enter the information needed on the first slide
- Create a new slide, deciding what will appear on it (e.g. text and a picture)
- Keep adding new slides until the slide show is complete
- Add digital effects to the slide show such as transition effects between slides (e.g. wipe or zoom)

Other presentation programs work in similar ways – with a series of slides on which is presented text, images, animations and sounds.

Creating a presentation using *PhotoStory3*

Presentations are created in *PhotoStory3* by following the prompts from a 'Wizard' which guides you through the process step by step.

The images needed for the story are loaded

The images are edited (if necessary)

Titles are added (if needed)

The effects are entered and the commentary is recorded

Background music is added (if required)

The story is saved as a video

Make sure the images for each group's story are saved into clearly labelled folders to make the loading of each set of images more straightforward.

(Optional) How to add callout speech bubbles to an image in a presentation

To add speech bubbles to a picture which has been loaded into *PowerPoint* you will need to use the Drawing toolbar. This can be accessed by clicking on **Toolbars** in the **View** menu and then clicking on **Drawing**.

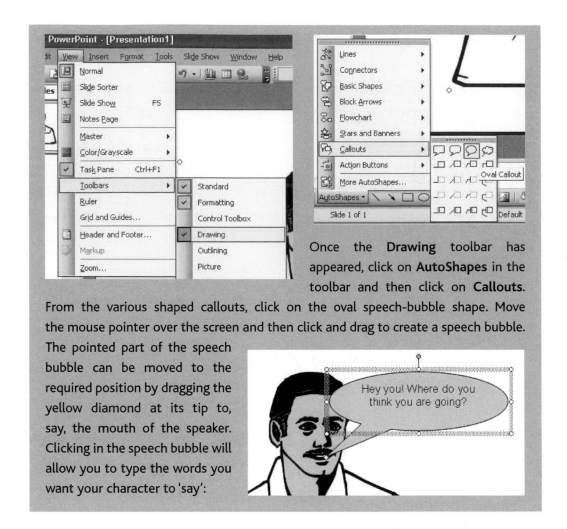

Once the **Drawing** toolbar has appeared, click on **AutoShapes** in the toolbar and then click on **Callouts**. From the various shaped callouts, click on the oval speech-bubble shape. Move the mouse pointer over the screen and then click and drag to create a speech bubble.

The pointed part of the speech bubble can be moved to the required position by dragging the yellow diamond at its tip to, say, the mouth of the speaker. Clicking in the speech bubble will allow you to type the words you want your character to 'say':

What will the children learn?

How to storyboard a photo-drama

The extent to which you let the children take control of this aspect will be dependent on how well you prepare them for this and how independent they are in creating their own plots. The drawings do not need to be more than stick people (give them the option of drawing or writing about what happens in each scene).

How to use a digital camera

Lower-cost cameras tend to be easier to use as they have fewer controls. You may have to anticipate the difficulties which the children may encounter and prepare them for solutions. Encourage the children to take more than one picture of a scene so they can be selective.

The importance of viewpoint

The most important skill to emphasise is the framing of the shot, hence the demonstration in the first activity to raise their awareness that viewpoint and distance from the action can affect the impact of the picture. You may want to give the children a preliminary practice task which enables them to experiment with framing their pictures. As a reminder, the suggested viewpoints are:

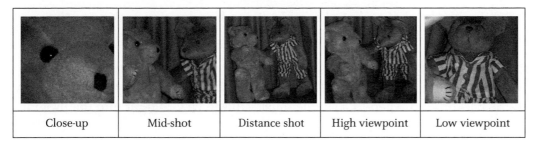

| Close-up | Mid-shot | Distance shot | High viewpoint | Low viewpoint |

Basic digital photo editing

As indicated above, the most useful editing feature is cropping, to enable the children to select the part of the image which communicates the story. Other features such as adjusting the brightness and colour are optional extras. Some photo-editing packages (including the editor in *PhotoStory*) include an auto-adjust option which optimises the colour and brightness settings as well as cropping.

How to create a simple linear presentation

Clearly, the most important aspect of a photo-story is sequencing and making sure that the various images tell a coherent story. Storyboarding helps to overcome this problem but, with digital imaging, if an additional scene needs to be created, it can be set up, shot and inserted in a few minutes. Presenting their half-completed stories to the rest of the class will very quickly pinpoint any gaps in the narrative.

How to evaluate a photo-drama

The first activity is important for helping the children to identify the criteria they will be using to evaluate their own and each other's stories. Without a clear set of criteria evaluations tend to lack focus and clarity and sometimes judgements become personalised and subjective. If you are concerned about the relationships between some of the children in the class, the evaluations can be completed on paper and you can vet the responses.

Challenging the more able and supporting the less able: modifying the project for older and younger pupils

Adjusting the expectations for storylines

Intervening during the planning or storyboarding stage by asking questions about the plot, characters and settings can help the children introduce more sophisticated storylines. For example, the end of the story in Activity 2 could show the bully being bullied by an older brother or a parent.

Children who lack the confidence to create their own story from scratch can be given a story to dramatise or a skeleton story (see above) to elaborate upon.

Adjusting the level of technical complexity and/or decision making to the presentation

PhotoStory3 enables the children to record their own commentary or dialogue to accompany each scene and it also allows a soundtrack to be played continuously in the background. There is a simple music-editing wizard built into the program or music from other sources can be inserted. Older or more experienced children could compose a piece of music using a music program and use this as the background. Alternatively, sound effects could be added to some scenes. If *PowerPoint* is used, a branching photo-story could be constructed (see Project 3).

If using *PowerPoint* or another similar presentation package, the learning curve for the children can be eased by providing them with a template file. For example, you could set up a presentation containing ten slides, each slide comprising a text box and an image. All the children then have to do is insert the image and write the accompanying dialogue in the text box. However, the more you set up for the children, the fewer opportunities are provided for the children to develop their ICT skills.

Adjusting the level of support (adult or peer)

Those providing support will need to be briefed on the purposes of each activity and the skills needed. Their role as guide rather than demonstrator will also need to be explained.

Why teach this?

When planning the story and setting up the scenes for the digital camera, you should ensure that the children are considering the visual communication of information. For example, will a close-up of a face portray more information than a mid-shot? When producing their presentations your interventions should aim to help the children make considered and informed decisions about the impact of each slide on their audience. How might the dialogue be made more realistic?

In addition to the evaluation activity, you should encourage children to discuss and share their ideas throughout the project. The aim is to help the children make productive use of the criteria they devise not only to evaluate the work of others but to improve the quality of their own work.

This project could act as a direct replacement for either QCA ICT Unit 4A: *Writing for different audiences* or Unit 6A: *Multimedia presentation* as it addresses many of the same learning objectives. It could also act as a bridge between Units 4A and 6A during Year 5.

A great advantage of computer-based tasks is that they can support real collaboration. Provided the groups are chosen carefully, opportunities are available for discussion and collaborative decision making in devising the story, staging the scenes and editing the presentation. In addition, to make the scenes look realistic the children should be encouraged to act them out. The skills required for plotting an effective story are reinforced by this project. Although it places little emphasis on descriptive writing, the project could be used to consolidate or introduce children to the conventions and structure of dialogue. For example, photo-dramas could be turned into illustrated books.

Visual literacy is considered to be an important part of children's education. Children are surrounded by information in a range of forms other than text, and hence teachers need to ensure that they have the skills and knowledge required to be able to make sense of this information. Margaret Meek (1991), for example, argues that 'new literacies develop new illiterates'. Some interesting studies (e.g. Long 1953; Pickford 2004) have revealed that young children tend to view images by focusing on specific details, whereas older children are more likely to remember the image as a whole. Making the shift from detail-specific to whole-scene perception of images is an important part of children's development. The most effective way to understand a medium of communication is to communicate with it. Creating their own visual presentations and focusing on the impact of various viewpoints to create different impressions should help children begin to appreciate how important it is to 'read' images carefully.

Related projects which make use of digital images in other subject contexts include: *Humanities* Project 9 (*A video of a visit to a place of worship*), *Humanities* Project 7 (*Link with a contrasting locality*), *Science* Project 3 (*Concept cartoons*), *Science* Project 7 (*Multimedia information source*) and *Arts* Project 5 (*Digital photos*).

References and further reading

Long, M. (1953) 'Children's reactions to geographical pictures', *Geography*, 180.

Meek, M. (1991) *On Being Literate*, London: The Bodley Head.

Pickford, A. (2004) *Graphicacy*, retrieved on 22/4/05 from www.pickford. abelgratis.co.uk

Project Fact Card: Project 8: Digital video

Who is it for?

- 9- to 10-year-olds (NC Levels 2–5)

What will the children do?

- The children use low-cost digital video cameras (or the video feature of a digital stills camera) to produce a 'magazine' article. The example described here is for a 'news' programme. After studying a news report from a television programme and identifying the key features and format, the children will plan, storyboard and script their own video news report. They will then film and edit the report. Finally, they will film the overall programme to link the reports together and evaluate the outcome

What should the children know already?

- How to use a word processor
- The sorts of topics which could be covered by a video report

What do I need to know?

- The basic features and structure of a TV news report
- How to script a TV news report
- How to use a digital video camera
- The terminology associated with filming
- How to use a digital video-editing software package
- (Optional) How to create a template document or writing frame for a word processor

What resources will I need?

- A report from a TV news programme
- A word processor
- (Optional) A template document for scripting or storyboarding
- Low-cost digital video cameras and associated video-editing software
- (Optional) A digital stills camera

What will the children learn?

- The basic features and structure of a TV news report
- How to script a TV news report
- How to evaluate the effectiveness of a TV news report
- How to use a digital video camera
- How to use a digital video-editing software package

How to challenge the more able

- Give them more control over the decision making
- Use a more sophisticated video camera and/or video-editing package

How to support the less able

- Provide them with a partially completed script, writing frame or skeleton script
- Give them a topic for their report
- Make a whole-class video report (with different groups assigned to specific roles)
- Provide more support (adult and/or peer)

Why teach this?

- It addresses ICT NC KS2 PoS statements 2a, 2b, 3a, 3b
- It complements QCA ICT Scheme of Work Units 6A (and 4A)
- It addresses English NC KS2 PoS statements En1, 1b–f, 3a, 3c–e, 4a, 4d, 5, 6a, 8a, 9a, 10a–c, 11a–c; En2, 5a–c, 5e, 5g, 9b, 9c; En3, 1a–e, 2a–c, 2f, 6a, 9b, 9c, 11, 12
- It complements NLS units for Year 5 Term 1 Sentences 4, 9; Texts 21, 24; Year 5 Term 2 Texts 14, 15, 22, 24; Year 5 Term 3 Texts (7), 13, 14, 15, 18, (19)
- It enhances the children's understanding of the role of the media in communicating information
- It introduces the notion of bias and selective use of information
- It introduces children to some of the conventions of TV and video production

Digital video

The project described here uses persuasive writing as the focus but it could be adapted to explore imaginative, descriptive or even instructional writing. In addition, the children could dramatise playscripts (or screenplays) they have written.

What will the children do?

Activity 1: Study a magazine article from a television programme to identify the key features and format

Record a suitable TV news report (see 'What resources will I need?', below) on video (or DVD).

After explaining the purpose and structure of the project and the ensuing activity, show the children the TV news report. Ask the children to comment on anything they have noticed about the way the report is presented. Questioning could focus on:

⊙ the topic being presented (e.g. was it interesting, was it understandable?);

⊙ the way the article is structured (i.e. what shots were used – e.g. presenter explains story to the camera, shot of the scene, interview with a witness/expert, another shot of the scene, interview continues, presenter sums up to camera, back to the studio);

⊙ the words used by the presenter (i.e. formal or informal register, technical vocabulary, recount, report).

Watch the video clip again focusing on any unanswered questions and asking them to note any details about the way the article is structured and presented. Remind them that they will be working on a report of their own and so need to study how it is done.

Split the children into groups and ask them to discuss and then feed back responses to the following:

- Did the way the article was presented make it interesting for the viewer – how?

- How did the presenter make sure the audience understood what was being presented?

- What sorts of words did s/he use?

- How did the presenter introduce and end the story?

- How many separate shots were used in the report?

- If you had presented this story, would you have changed any part of it?

The groups report back and compare notes. If necessary, the video could be shown again to resolve any disputes or differences of opinion. Although it depends on the report being shown, children (and many adults) are often surprised by the number of different shots used in even a short report. You might find it useful to have checked the number yourself. At the end of the plenary reinforce the key ideas for this activity:

- News reports are short and highly focused but convey a lot of information

- A number of shots are used to ensure the viewers understand

- The presenter uses mostly formal language

Activity 2: Plan, storyboard and script their own video news reports

Remind the children about the news report viewed in the previous activity (you might show it again). Explain the purposes and structure of this activity; the children will be planning and scripting their own report for a class 'News' programme.

Organise the children into editorial teams of four. The choice of topic for each group could be discussed or allocated, depending on circumstances. Assuming the focus is on persuasive writing, a series of local and/or national themes could be chosen:

- Parking outside the school (one group presenting the case for, one against)
- School uniform
- School dinners
- SATs tests
- Compulsory sports for all
- Pocket money
- Litter
- Graffiti, etc.

Alternatively, the children could prepare news reports about the school and its work. Assuming there are eight groups the stories could be allocated as follows:

- Foundation/Reception class news
- Year 1 news
- Year 2 news, etc.
- Sports reports

Explain the process of planning the news item and the terminology they should use. At this point it would be useful to decide on the 'anchor(s)' – the presenter(s) in the 'studio' who will introduce each news report. This could be the teacher or decided by popular vote. Knowing the identity of the anchor(s) will enable the presenters of the news reports to include linking statements such as '*Thanks, Ted. Yes, here we are in the playground*' and '*And now back to Mary in the studio*'.

The children work in groups to plan and script their news item. They need to decide on their roles (camera operator, presenter(s), interviewee(s)), the location for the 'shoot', the structure of the report (e.g. introduction by presenter to camera, establishing shots, interview, summing up). The report then needs to be scripted and/or storyboarded.

In the plenary, each group provides a progress report for feedback and suggestions.

Activity 3: Film the reports

Explain and demonstrate the operation of the camera. Shooting, downloading and viewing one group's introduction to their report is a useful way of showing how the system works. It is important to discuss and explain the shooting criteria. Suggested criteria are:

⊙ Can you hear the speaker(s)?

⊙ Is the shot framed well?

⊙ Is the camera steady?

If time permits, you should give the children a familiarisation task before they film their piece. This could be to film the presenter's introduction on location. They then upload this to the computer editing package and evaluate it using the criteria.

The organisation for the filming will be dependent on the availability of equipment. If there are sufficient cameras and computers for each group to work at the same time, the filming could be done in one lesson. However, if there are a limited number of cameras, then the filming will have to be done on a rolling rota. Uploading the clips to the computer(s) again will be dependent on the system used and the number of computers with the relevant software installed. It is useful for the children to view the clips as soon as possible after the filming to evaluate them. If necessary, they may have to film some shots again.

Activity 4: Edit the reports

Once the clips have been shot and uploaded to the computer(s), you can demonstrate the editing process.

The groups edit their clips but at this stage they should not be exported or rendered until they have been evaluated by the rest of the class (and you).

In a plenary session, the reports are shown and evaluated using the criteria defined in the first activity. Feedback is given with comments being either 'praise' or 'suggestion'.

Activity 5: Film the overall programme, linking the reports together

Once all the reports are completed, the 'anchor' links can be scripted and filmed. The scripting could be done by you or partly by the whole class as a shared writing task. The anchor link comments need only be a few sentences and could be unscripted but this will be dependent on the capabilities of those playing the role(s) of the anchor(s).

The filming of the anchor links could be done with the whole class present, as group work or as an after-school activity. The final editing of the whole programme could be carried out by a group of 'expert' children or by you as 'homework'.

Activity 6: Evaluate the outcome

Once the complete programme has been compiled it is shown to the whole class and/or an invited audience. This will require two 'screenings' – the first to allow the children to enjoy the programme as 'entertainment' and the second to enable them to evaluate the programme more objectively.

The children should be asked to suggest criteria which could be used to evaluate the various news items, such as:

⊙ Technical – the filming and sound are clear and effective

⊙ Content – the information is presented clearly and informatively

⊙ Presentation – the report is well structured

⊙ Argument – the case for/against the topic is convincing

During the second screening the film is paused after each report to allow the children to complete an individual evaluation. These can be in the form of a simple score card (a copy of which can be found on the CD-ROM accompanying this book):

Presentation:_____

	Very good	Good	OK	Not sure
Technical				
Content				
Presentation				
Argument				

Depending on the relationships in the class, you could either have the children discussing their feedback for each report or ask the children to identify the report they considered to be the most effective in each category. The final discussion should focus on ways of improving the outcome if the activity were to be repeated.

What should the children know already?

How to use a word processor

If you want the children to word process their scripts or storyboards, they should have a working knowledge of the features of a word processor. The focus for this project is on digital video and hence the word processing is merely a means to an end.

The sorts of topics which could be covered by a video report

The children will inevitably be familiar with TV news reports but may not have studied them carefully. In preparation for the project you could ask them to do some homework in watching news reports carefully to be able to describe their structure and the sorts of topics they cover.

What resources will I need?

A report from a TV news programme

News reports are ideal for this type of activity as they tend to be short and highly focused. The news report can be either recorded off-air (using a video or DVD recorder) or downloaded from the TV company's website. The content of the report should be appropriate for the age group of the children and could relate to a topic being studied. A report from a children's news or magazine programme could be used, for example. A 'location' report is usually visually more interesting than a studio-based report. Ensure the report has a clearly defined structure (e.g. presenter introduces item to camera, establishing shot of the location, interview with witness or expert, presenter sums up to camera and links back to the studio).

A word processor

(Optional) A template document for scripting or storyboarding

If you want the children to script their report, a word processor template or writing frame could be prepared to ensure the children's reports have a clearly defined structure enabling them to be linked with the main programme (see opposite). An example template has been provided on the CD-ROM that comes with this book.

Low-cost digital video cameras and associated video-editing software

(Optional) A digital stills camera

The price of digital video cameras has fallen steadily in recent years and hence it is possible for a school to buy several cameras for a relatively modest sum. An even

News report about: _____

Authors: _____   _____

_____   _____

Introduction

Thank you _____. This is _____ reporting from
_____. An important feature of the debate about _____
is _____.

As can be seen _____.

Interview

A person who is particularly affected by this issue is _____ who
has _____ .

Could you tell us how you feel about _____ ?
What do you think about the views held by others who claim _____.
How would you respond to _____ ?
What do you feel is the most important feature?
And finally, _____ ?

Conclusion

And so it would seem that _____.
_____ suggests that the most important thing to consider is
_____.
This is _____ reporting from
_____. And now back to _____ in the
studio.

more cost effective approach is to invest in low-cost digital cameras such as the *Digital Movie Creator* (DMC) marketed by TAG Developments. These cameras and the editing software are designed specifically for use in schools. For less than £800, ten DMCs can be purchased providing enough for all groups to have their own camera and the software installed on a computer.

Low-cost cameras such as the DMC will often include a simple video-editing package. However, a free alternative if you have Windows XP is *Windows Movie Maker 2*. If you have an early version of XP you can upgrade *Windows Movie Maker 1* by visiting the Microsoft website. iMac users should have *Apple iMovie* installed as standard.

What do I need to know?

The basic features and structure of a TV news report

The structure of news reports does vary but basically they comprise an introduction from the presenter to camera, sometimes accompanied by some establishing shots of the location, then the main part which may include an interview with an expert or witness, then a conclusion in which the presenter sums up the key issues to the camera and hands back to the studio.

How to script a TV news report

The writing frame could be used as the basis for the presenter's script. Alternatively, you could produce a simplified version of a full script which includes directions for the camera and sound crew. Examples of news scripts can be found by searching the internet. Alternatively, you can download *MS Word* templates for creating scripts from the BBC website: http://www.bbc.co.uk/writersroom/writing/ or get a free complete program for scriptwriting from http://www.mindstarprods.com/cinergy/ScriptEditor.html. Guidance on writing effective news scripts can be found at: http://aee3070.ifas.ufl.edu/Writing.htm

For more information on scripting, see Croton (1986).

How to use a digital video camera

There is more to using a video camera than simply pointing and pressing the record button. Here is a simple three-point *aide-mémoire* to improving the children's use of a camera:

⊙ *Sound:* The microphone is on the camera and hence the children need to consider the distance between the presenter, interviewee(s) and the camera, and background noise (e.g. from a road or the playground) when filming.

⊙ *Vision:* The framing of the shot is important. The Rule of Thirds suggests that if the screen is divided into thirds, then the most important part of a scene should be on one of these lines:

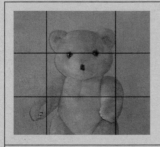	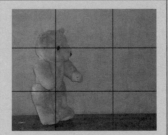	
The focus for an image should coincide with at least one of the thirds	Or even two of the thirds	But attention should be drawn into the scene, not out of it

⊙ *Movement:* Keep the camera still or steady and only move or zoom if it is absolutely essential.

The terminology associated with filming

Although not essential, the children will enjoy using some of the terminology. Examples include:

- Shoot – a filming event
- Close-up – a shot in which a person's face or object fills the frame
- Mid-shot – a shot showing the waist up
- Long-shot – a shot showing the whole person
- Establishing shot – a view of the whole scene (usually a long-shot) helping the viewer understand where the scene is being filmed
- Two-shot/Three-shot – a shot with two/three people in view (e.g. an interview)
- Track – the camera follows the movement of the people in the scene
- Zoom – the camera moves in closer or further away from the scene
- Pan – the camera moves across a scene

How to use a digital video-editing software package

Most video-editing packages are easy to use but will take a little practice. The basic features are a *library of clips* which can be dragged on to a *storyboard* to make the video. The video can be *previewed* at any time. Once the scenes have been assembled, they can be trimmed to remove unwanted segments and *digital effects* can be added to move from one scene to the next, for example. Some editors allow you also to edit the soundtrack and to insert or record new sounds, such as a voice-over.

(Optional) How to create a template document or writing frame for a word processor

Word processors such as *MS Word* enable the user to create template documents which cannot be accidentally overwritten. When saving the template, select **Document Template (*.dot)** from the **Save as type:** pull-down list in the **Save As ...** dialogue box:

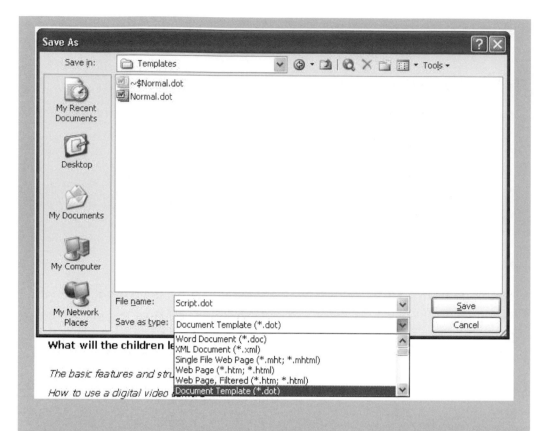

What will the children le

The basic features and stru

How to use a digital video

Alternatively, you can protect a document from being overwritten by making it 'Read-only'. Once a document has been saved, right click on its icon and select **Properties** from the pop-up menu. Click the **Read-only** checkbox and then click **OK**.

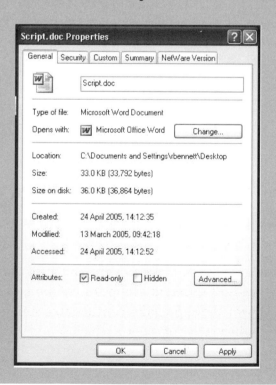

What will the children learn?

The basic features and structure of a TV news report

How to script a TV news report

How to evaluate the effectiveness of a TV news report

The use of a template or writing frame will help the children appreciate the structure of a report. Using criteria which are clear and explicit should ensure that evaluations are well focused and fair.

How to use a digital video camera

Creating their own video should help the children understand the way in which TV reports are devised and also how the presentation of a story can affect the way the information is portrayed. This aspect should form an important part of the final plenary when children reflect on the effectiveness of their own reports and how these compare to those they have seen on the television.

How to use a digital video-editing software package

In addition to the skills required to edit their video clips, the children will be learning how the sequencing of shots can affect the way information is presented and that a news report has many similarities to any narrative writing – a good story (written or filmed) has an interesting start, a well-detailed middle and a conclusion which reminds us what has happened. When asked what advice he would give to a student hoping to become successful in television, David Brinkley, a leading US TV presenter, replied: 'Three things: learn to write, learn to write and learn to write.'

Challenging the more able and supporting the less able: modifying the project for older and younger pupils

Adjusting the amount of decision making involved

The level of detail in the content of the writing frame or template script can be adjusted to suit the needs of different groups of children, even within the same class. The example shown above provides considerable support and, if used with every group, will result in a series of reports which sound very similar.

Older or more experienced children should have the confidence and the competence to make more decisions. They could discuss and choose their own topic(s) and organise the way in which the background information is gathered. Rather than having a writing frame for their scripts, they could study several news reports (e.g. by accessing them from a TV website) and then produce their own.

Matching the complexity of the equipment and software to the experience of the children

Although increasing the level of technicality is not necessarily the most effective way of adding more challenge to an ICT-based activity, some of the most basic video-editing packages restrict what the children can achieve. Some, for example, do not allow the soundtrack from one video clip to be copied to another clip. This technique is very useful for news reporting when, for example, an interview needs to be edited. Rather than cutting out a section of an interview and leaving an obvious 'jump-cut', a 'cut-away' shot of a background shot can be used to cover the edit. This can only be achieved with a more sophisticated video-editing software package.

If resources and time are seriously restricted, then the whole class could work together on a single report. The script could be produced through shared writing and the report could include interviews from several interested parties. The teacher can therefore be in control of most if not all of the children's work.

Adjusting the level of support (adult and/or peer)

Anyone providing support will need to be well briefed in the purposes and structure of the tasks and the use of the equipment, but also be advised on how to provide guidance and explanation rather than acting as a demonstrator.

Why teach this?

The National Curriculum Programme of Study and Level descriptions do not specify precisely what children should be able to do with digital video. However, considering the needs of the audience and communicating information clearly and unambiguously is no less important for video than it is for written text. The advantage of the video is that the children can see the impact of their work on others (delighted applause is usually the spontaneous result).

This project provides ample opportunities for children to develop aspects of speaking and listening. Working in groups to develop their scripts requires them to discuss, evaluate each other's ideas and justify their choices. Role playing through the dramatisation of the news reports enables them to use formal language in a rigorous setting and to evaluate the effectiveness of their own performance and the performance of others.

As each news item will only last two or three minutes, the entire report could be scripted. Alternatively, some groups may prefer to prepare an outline script, with some parts written in full detail and others little more than a series of headings. It will be worth while watching several news reports before the children script their own to identify some of the key features. Guidance provided by the Radio-Television News Directors Association (www.rtnda.org) suggests that news reports should:

⊙ use the active voice – subject, verb, object;

⊙ recognise that nouns and verbs are stronger than adjectives and adverbs;

- avoid jargon and technical words – keep it simple;

- include defining details such as the make of car, the name of the interviewee, the name of the town;

- tell the story as if to a friend (e.g. 'This may seem hard to believe but . . .');

- be rehearsed several times to check it works before performing on camera;

- explain what the viewer is being shown – even if it is obvious.

Writing successful news reports takes years of experience and training. The reports the children write are likely to be flawed, but with support and guidance (e.g. through writing frames) and through analysing the content and structure of recorded news reports they may gain some insight into how the news is reported – and how different viewpoints can be represented by the selective use of information.

See also *Humanities* Project 7 (*Link with a contrasting locality*), *Science* Project 8 (*Digital video – freeze frame*) and *Arts* Project 10 (*Creating a digital 'silent film'*) for related activities.

References and further reading

Croton, G. (1986) *From Script to Screen: Documentaries*, Borehamwood: BBC Television Training.

Project Fact Card: Project 9: Creating an information website

Who is it for?

- 10- to 11-year-olds (NC Levels 3–6)

What will the children do?

- They will gather information about authors and poets from various sources but principally from the internet. They will evaluate the design of web pages and then design and produce their own web pages, presenting information about authors and poets and their work. They will then combine and link their web pages to produce a website and evaluate the effectiveness of their website in comparison to others

What should the children know already?

- How to use the internet, books and CD-ROM information sources to find information
- How to use a word processor

What do I need to know?

- How to search the internet
- How to create and export bookmarks/Favorites
- How to design and create web pages
- How to create a website with hyper-linked pages

What resources will I need?

- Access to the internet
- A web browser
- A bookmark list of websites and web pages for evaluation
- A program for creating web pages

What will the children learn?

- How to search for, access and extract information from books, the internet and/or CD-ROMs
- Background information about authors and poets
- How to present information for a potential worldwide audience
- (Optional) How to identify and replicate the style of a particular author or poet
- How to evaluate the effectiveness of a web page and a website
- How to design and create a web page
- (Some children) How to hyperlink web pages

How to challenge the more able

- Create the hyperlinks between pages
- Design and create the home page for a website
- Create a series of linked pages portraying different sorts of information about a particular author or poet

How to support the less able

- Provide a template document or writing frame for the web page
- Provide a set of bookmark links to websites which have been checked for content
- Provide more support

Why teach this?

- It addresses ICT NC KS2 PoS statements 1a–c, 2a, 2b, 3a, 3b
- It complements QCA ICT Scheme of Work Units 6D, 6A, 5C
- It addresses English NC KS2 PoS statements En1, 3a–c; En2, 3a–e, 9b; En3, 2a, 2c–f, 7d, 11, 12
- It complements NLS units for Year 6 Term 1 Texts 12, 13, 14, 17, 18; Year 6 Term 3 Texts 17, 18, 19, 20, 21, 22

Creating an information website

Although the project described here relates to Year 6, it could readily be adapted for any age group or topic in Key Stage 2.

What will the children do?

Activity 1: Gather information about authors and poets from various sources

Discuss an author or poet with whom the children are familiar, focusing on information about personal background and the writer's work. Ask the children to list other poets or writers with whom they are familiar. Discuss how they might find more information about these writers.

Ask the children to compile a list of questions or headings which will form the focus for their enquiries. For example, the headings might include:

⊙ Full name

⊙ Picture(s)

⊙ Life story

⊙ Likes/Dislikes

⊙ First book/poem

⊙ Overview of work and style(s) of writing

⊙ Your favourite book/story/poem

Remind the children about how to search for information using books, the internet and CD-ROM encyclopaedia and demonstrate how to create a folder of bookmarks.

Allocate the children to pairs and identify an author or poet for each group. Tell them they need to find information about their writer using books, CD-ROMs and the internet. They should bookmark any websites they find to enable them to use the information later. At this stage all they need do is make a note of what information can be found where.

In the plenary, the children compare notes on the sources which yielded the best information and share with each other any information which might be useful (e.g. general websites about children's writers). Make a note of websites which children feel are particularly useful.

Activity 2: Evaluate the design of web pages

Remind them about the websites they mentioned in the previous activity which they had identified as being particularly useful. Show these to the class and ask them to identify the features which they feel make them 'good'. For example, they may suggest:

- *Content* – the information is appropriate for answering their questions. The information seems to be accurate and up to date

- *Presentation* – the information is clearly presented and easy to read

- *Design* – the website is attractive and interesting. Effective use is made of colour, images and icons

- *Navigability* – it is easy to find the information they need

- *Audience* – the style of writing and presentation is appropriate for children

List features they have identified as the basis for the evaluation criteria they will use to 'score' the websites they bookmarked and others which you have identified. The children work in pairs to evaluate the effectiveness of websites, scoring each on a five-point scale on the criteria you have agreed.

In the plenary, discuss their evaluations. Start with websites which anyone has identified as having a maximum or very high rating. Look also at websites which have a low rating. Discuss the features of an 'ideal' website and web page.

Activity 3: Design and produce web pages presenting information about authors and poets and their work

NOTE: This activity may take more than one lesson to complete.

Remind them of the websites they had identified as being particularly effective. Explain the purpose of the activity – they will be creating their own web pages containing information about the writers they have been researching. Demonstrate how to create a web page and outline the essential content. For example, you could use the questions generated in Activity 1 as subheadings.

The children work in pairs to create a web page of information about their writer – taking account of the features they had identified in the previous activity.

In the plenary, the children share what they have learned about creating good websites.

Activity 4: Combine and link their web pages to produce a website

The organisation of this activity will depend on the availability of computers and the skills and confidence of the children. At some point all the children's completed web pages, together with accompanying images, will have to be transferred to one 'master' computer (e.g. via the network or a portable memory stick).

You could ask one group to prepare the home page for the website with links to each web page created by the children. This should be saved to the master computer. Through the course of a week, each pair could create a link from the home page to their web page. Alternatively, you could create the website for them.

Activity 5: Evaluate the effectiveness of their website in comparison with others

Remind the children of the criteria they used to evaluate websites in Activity 2 and then explain this activity.

The children work in pairs to evaluate their author website. They could be instructed to evaluate at least two other pages and their own page, scoring them on a four-point scale against each criterion.

The pairs are invited to share with the rest of the class the web page which they felt scored the highest and suggest ways in which they could have improved their own web page.

What should the children know already?

How to use the internet, books and CD-ROM information sources to find information

This project could be used to introduce or consolidate the children's skills in searching for, accessing and extracting information. If they are unfamiliar with copying and pasting text and images from the internet or CD-ROMs, this will need to be demonstrated as part of Activity 3. Similarly, some children may need to be shown or reminded about note taking from books or CD-ROMs which do not support copying and pasting.

How to use a word processor

Some word processors can be used to create web pages and so the only additional skills needed by the children will be in creating hyperlinks and saving a document as a web page. Dedicated web-authoring software such as *Microsoft FrontPage* requires very little additional instruction although the positioning of images on a page may need to be demonstrated.

What resources will I need?

Access to the internet

To evaluate websites, the children will need a computer suite which can access the internet. The website evaluation activity can be carried out on a single classroom computer but this will clearly take longer and will require a rolling rota of pairs. Each pair will need a minimum of 30 minutes for website evaluation but preferably an hour. Some children could continue the web-based tasks at home but it might be advisable to give them a briefing sheet on internet safety (see the *DfES Superhighway Safety* website: www.safety.ngfl.gov.uk).

A web browser (e.g. *Internet Explorer*, *Opera*, *Netscape*, *Firefox*)

Most computers have *Internet Explorer* installed as the standard web browser. However, other web browsers such as *Netscape*, *Opera* and *Firefox* provide additional tools for browsing (such as multiple tab windows) and are less prone to virus attack.

A bookmark list of websites and web pages for evaluation

If you feel that the focus for this activity should lie with website evaluation and/or the creation of web pages, you may decide to by-pass the searching and provide the children with a prepared list of websites which you have found and checked beforehand. This can save time and ensure the websites they evaluate include the features you want them to consider. For example, some websites which the children rate highly may include animated characters or movie clips which are beyond the scope of their own web-authoring skills.

A program for creating web pages (e.g. *MS FrontPage*, *MS Word*, *MS Publisher*, *Textease*, *Granada Writer v3*)

Most word processors and some desktop publishing packages will allow you to create web pages. Usually an option is included in the **File** menu to save the current document as a web page.

However, word-processing and desktop publishing software is not primarily designed for creating web pages and hence compromises are made. Often, images presented on the web page are shifted and sometimes the spaces between paragraphs or blocks of text change. While this is usually no more than a minor irritation, at times it can be extremely frustrating – particularly if children want to create a particular effect or impression with the positioning of objects on the screen. Website creation programs such as *FrontPage*, *WebEditor* (Namo) and *BlackCat Spider* are little more difficult to use than word processors but allow greater control over the final appearance of the web page.

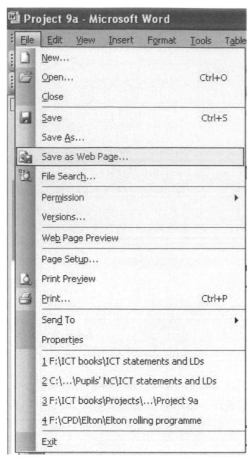

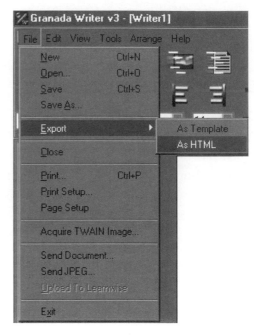

Export as HTML (i.e. a web document) in Granada Writer v3

Save as Web Page . . . in Ms Word

What do I need to know?

How to search the internet

You need to be able to show the children how to narrow their searches through the inclusion of more specific search terms, searches on searches and the use of advanced search tools. There is a booklet on the CD-ROM accompanying this book which gives more guidance on improving the efficiency of web searching. This can be adapted for use by the children if required.

How to create and export bookmarks/Favorites

As a teacher, knowing how to manage bookmarks is extremely useful. In Activity 1 the children will need to create their own folders of bookmark links or as indicated above you could provide them with a prepared and carefully selected set of bookmarks. The children could also include links to external websites in their own web pages. (Refer to the booklet on the CD-ROM.)

How to design and create web pages

You need only to search the internet for information on 'web page design' to see how much guidance there is (and also how views differ) on the design of effective web pages. In addition to gathering information from the internet you might want to use this list of features as a starting point for guiding the children's web designing:

- Keep it simple and clear
- Use the same font for the page
- Use headings to help readers find the information they need
- Leave space
- Use images but only if they are relevant

How to create a website with hyperlinked pages

As indicated above, word processors can be used to create web pages but to link all the children's pages together and create a home page you will probably find a web-authoring package far more reliable and effective. *Microsoft FrontPage* is very easy to use but may not have been included with your PC as standard. Some web-authoring programs can be downloaded free of charge from the internet. One of the most popular is *HotHTML 2001* which can be downloaded from www.wsoftware.biz

Creating hyperlinks

Before creating hyperlinks between web pages it is essential to make sure all the separate web pages, together with any image files included on those pages, are brought together and saved on one computer, preferably in the same folder. You may have noticed when web pages load into your computer that sometimes the images appear more slowly than the text. Unlike word-processed documents, images on a web page are not embedded in the document. When an image is included on a web page, rather than the image becoming an integral part of the page, a link is created from the web page to the image file. Thus, when the web page is loaded on a computer, the computer has to follow the link to where the image is saved and insert it into the page. If the link cannot be followed, then the image cannot be loaded. When a word processor such as *Word* or *Textease* saves a document as a web page it will create a separate folder containing all the images. If the web page is transferred to another computer, the folder needs to be copied as well otherwise the images will not be saved.

If you lack confidence or are inexperienced with creating web pages our advice is to get the children to create their web pages using a word processor and save them as a word processor document. Once all these documents have been transferred to a folder on your 'master' computer, you or the children can save them as web pages in the same 'master' folder. The home page for the website can then be created and all the hyperlinks made to the various web pages. Although compromises will need to be made on the appearance of some of the children's web pages, this approach should be more successful.

To create hyperlinks in *MS Word*

Highlight the text or the image you want to use as the link and then right click and select **Hyperlink . . .** or select **Hyperlink . . .** from the **Insert** menu:

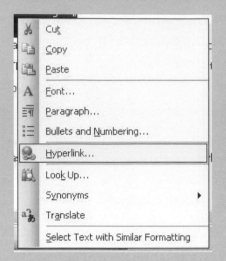

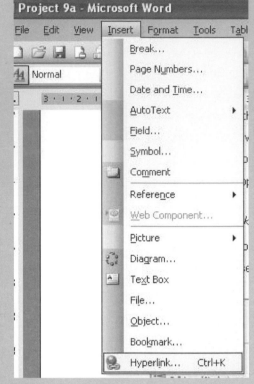

Locate the file to which you want the hyperlink created and then click **Open**. Save the document and then test the hyperlink by holding down the **Ctrl** (Control) key and clicking on the link. Once the document is saved as a web page the hyperlink should work as on a normal web page. To create a link to a web page on the internet, copy the address from the address pane in the web browser and then paste it (by holding down the **Ctrl** key and typing a **V**) into the **Address** box in the **Insert Hyperlink** dialogue box.

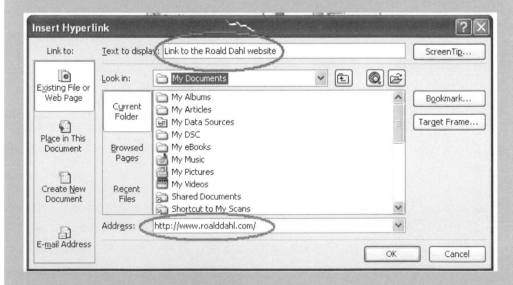

Creating a hyperlink with *Granada Writer v3*

Highlight the text, text box or image which will act as the link and then click on the **Make Link** button:

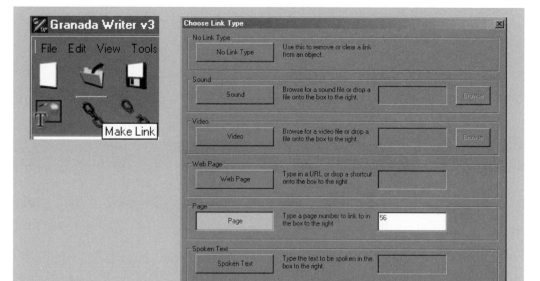

Click on the button beneath the type of link you want to create. Use **Browse** to locate the file to which you want to create a link, or copy or type the URL, page number or spoken text into the relevant field and then click the **OK** button.

NOTE: Other word processors and most web-authoring packages use a similar process for creating hyperlinks as one of the above.

What will the children learn?

How to search for, access and extract information from books, the internet and/or CD-ROMs

This project can be used to develop or consolidate children's knowledge and skills in:

⊙ improving the efficiency and accuracy of their web searching;

⊙ enhancing their ability to check the reliability and plausibility of information on websites;

⊙ developing their ability to copy and paste and rework text and images garnered from web pages;

⊙ extracting information from CD-ROM sources;

⊙ improving their skills in note taking from printed sources.

Background information about authors and poets

Giving the children a set of headings or questions will not only ensure the information contained on their own web pages will be comparable; it will help to focus their information gathering and encourage the application of skimming, scanning and keyword searching for relevant information.

How to present information for a potential worldwide audience

In most classroom-based activities the audience for the children's work is primarily the teacher, occasionally the rest of the class, at times their parents and from time to time the rest of the school. Potentially, the audience for web pages is global. Once the web pages have been created and checked, they could readily be uploaded to the school's website. Taking account of the needs, interests and background of an internet audience makes this type of activity purposeful and very real.

(Optional) How to identify and replicate the style of a particular author or poet

To complement Activity 3, the children could write a paragraph or poem in the style of their chosen author and include this as an item on their web page.

How to evaluate the effectiveness of a web page and a website

The great virtue of evaluating web pages and websites is not only that it will help inform the design and production of the children's own web pages; it will help them become more discerning and constructively critical when searching the internet for information. Moreover, it enables them to appreciate what it is like to become a creator of information as well as a receiver of others' ideas.

How to design and create a web page

While the practical skills involved in the creation of web pages and websites are little more complex than word processing, the design of effective web pages for the efficient communication of information in a multimedia environment is an important area which this project touches upon. The knowledge and understanding addressed by this project lay the foundation for a diverse and important aspect of communication.

(Some children) How to hyperlink web pages

The concept of hyperlinking is fundamental to multimedia. The ability to identify and create links between information and ideas within and across domains is similar to the way in which the human mind works. By creating a range of different ways in which users can access information the notion is that it will appeal to all types of learner with a multitude of background experiences.

Challenging the more able and supporting the less able: modifying the project for older and younger pupils

Adjusting the level of challenge in creating the web pages to match the children's capabilities

Those with more experience could be allocated the task of creating the home page and interlinking the pages. If there are several groups of children who are experienced or confident users of ICT, they could distribute the information about their chosen writer over several web pages and create their own hyperlinks between the pages. Some could even be given the responsibility of deciding the content for each web page.

Younger or more inexperienced users of ICT could be provided with templates or writing frames which takes over some of the decision making and reduces the amount of new learning required.

Providing a set of bookmark links to websites which have been checked for content

To remove the need for children to search for appropriate websites and also to gain some consensus on the effectiveness of different websites, you could prepare a bookmark list which could be imported into the web browser on each computer or you could prepare a simple web page with hyperlinks to the various pre-selected websites.

Matching the level of support to the needs of the children

Whether the support is provided by peers or adults, it is important they are well briefed not only in the content of the support needed but also in the method of delivery of the support. Support should primarily be in the form of explanation and guidance rather than demonstration.

Why teach this?

In this project, the children will be using the internet and CD-ROM sources to find things out. It is important that, when accessing websites, they consider the validity and accuracy of the information that they contain. They might, for example, find that two websites give conflicting information about an author. They should then be encouraged to decide which website they consider to be the most reliable.

Once information has been located on a website it can be copied and pasted into a document which will form the basis for the web page. To follow the agreed structure for the presentation of information on their web page the children will need to edit and amend the information they have downloaded. Repurposing information is a key skill which needs to be taught and reinforced.

In addition to developing their ideas through the manipulation of downloaded information, some children will be creating hyperlinks. Creating a web link is a form of programming – when a user clicks on a link, something happens (i.e. a new page or a website is loaded into the computer). Hyperlinking is a very important concept and skill which forms the basis for all forms of multimedia and hence this aspect of the project needs to be taught carefully and given due emphasis.

The presentation of information via a web page provides a means of emphasising for children the importance of ensuring the information they are communicating is clear and unambiguous – as the potential audience is world wide. Assuming the school has a website on which classes can post information, it should be possible to upload the web pages which the children have created to the World Wide Web. You may have to seek guidance from the school's ICT co-ordinator and check with the school's IT policy before transferring the information to the web.

This project can be used as a direct replacement for both QCA ICT Unit 6A: *Multimedia presentation* and Unit 6D: *Using the internet to search large databases and to interpret information*. Most of the learning objectives featured in both units are addressed by this project in a meaningful and relevant context. If the children's web pages are placed on the school's internet site, then the added incentive of writing for a potential worldwide audience should help to motivate the children into considering the content of their work carefully.

The learning objectives for QCA ICT Unit 5C: *Evaluating information, checking accuracy and questioning plausibility* are also addressed comprehensively through this project and hence this project could replace Unit 5C or build upon the knowledge and skills acquired.

The principal literacy foci of this project are: accessing information through searching, skimming and scanning; and evaluating the relevance of information and then editing text and information for presentation to others.

There are opportunities for them to practise their speaking and listening skills when working with others to decide on the format for the website they will ultimately produce and in expressing considered and informed judgements about the effectiveness of their own and others' web pages.

They will have opportunities to employ and develop a range of reading strategies by skimming through web-based information to find that which is most relevant to their enquiries. They will be required to make decisions about the accuracy and currency of the web-based information they acquire, particularly if there is conflicting information about their chosen author or poet presented on different websites.

Teachers have concerns about children copying and pasting information from the internet without comprehending its content. It is very important that the structure for the information on their web pages is clearly communicated and that the children appreciate they will have to rework, edit and integrate information from various sources into a coherent and cohesive whole. By reading examples of information texts on different websites they should begin to appreciate the styles used and the importance of linking ideas presented in different paragraphs. One way of doing this for those who lack experience is to give each paragraph a subheading which could be in the form of a question. These headings could be retained for the final draft or deleted.

Project Fact Card: Project 10: A *Macbeth* webquest

Who is it for?

- 10- to 11-year-olds (NC Levels 3–6)

What will the children do?

- Using a webquest, they work in 'production' teams to design a *PowerPoint* (or similar) presentation aimed at persuading a group of film company shareholders that their idea for a modern adaptation of *Macbeth* is worth investment. To prepare for the presentation they gather background information about the play and other people's adaptations; they then storyboard the play (either through drawings or through enactments shot with a digital stills camera). They compile their presentation and show this to the rest of the class who then decide (by secret ballot) which film is worth investment

What should the children know already?

- What a presentation is and how a good presentation is structured
- Some background knowledge of Shakespeare and an outline of the story of *Macbeth*

What do I need to know?

- How to structure and manage a webquest
- How to create presentations using *PowerPoint* (or similar)
- The features of an effective presentation

What resources will I need?

- Internet access and a computer suite and/or classroom computers
- A webquest (an example is provided on the CD-ROM that comes with this book)
- A list of appropriate websites containing the information needed by the children
- *PowerPoint* or a similar presentation program
- An example of a 'good' presentation

What will the children learn?

- How to locate, identify and access information on the internet to address specific lines of enquiry
- How to structure information as part of a collaborative project
- How to present information using ICT

How to challenge the more able

- Increase the level of challenge in the webquest tasks or make them more open ended
- Increase the level of demand for the quality and content of the presentation

How to support the less able

- Reduce the level of challenge in the webquest tasks
- Structure the presentation (e.g. with a template)
- Provide more support

Why teach this?

- It addresses ICT NC KS2 PoS statements 1a–c, 2a, 3a, 3b
- It complements ICT QCA Scheme of Work Units 5C, 6A, 6D
- It addresses English NC KS2 PoS statements En1, 3a–c; En2, 3a–e, 9b; En3, 2a, 2c–f, 7d, 11, 12
- It complements NLS units for Year 6 Term 1 Texts 12, 13, 14, 17, 18; Year 6 Term 3 Texts 17, 18, 19, 20, 21, 22

A *Macbeth* webquest

Webquests could theoretically be structured for any age group in Key Stage 2, but you would need to structure the project and scaffold the learning more carefully for younger pupils.

What will the children do?

Preliminary activity: Familiarisation with the story of *Macbeth*

If the play is the focus for literacy work, then the children may already be very familiar with the story. However, if they are coming to this activity 'cold', you should ensure they have sufficient knowledge of the story to be able to work on the project. This could be done by reading them a précis of the story or showing them a film version. The Polanski film is, however, somewhat gruesome and not appropriate for children. The animated version (*Shakespeare – The Animated Tales: Macbeth* (1992)) is more appropriate and lasts only 30 minutes.

Activity 1: Search the internet for information about adaptations of *Macbeth*

If the children are unfamiliar with webquests, the project needs to be introduced carefully to engage their interest and channel their enthusiasm. Explain how over the years different versions of *Macbeth* have been produced – if necessary, show them some of the examples using the web links in the webquest (see 'What resources will I need?', below).

Split the children into groups to begin searching the websites and gathering the information they need for the presentation. Towards the end of the session, the children will need time to share what they have found with the rest of their group and make decisions about the form their version of the play will take.

Activity 2: *PowerPoint* workshop

After showing the children the example of a *PowerPoint* presentation, demonstrate the basic features sufficient for them to create slides.

In their groups, the children decide on the design for their presentation and allocate the roles for the production of the initial slides, as specified in the webquest.

The children will need to be provided with some means of combining the slides they have produced on separate computers into a single presentation. If the school has a network, the separate presentations can be saved in a common folder and each slide can then be copied and pasted into the 'master' presentation. Alternatively, the presentations can be saved on to floppy disks or portable 'pen' drives and transferred to the master computer.

Activity 3: Storyboarding their adaptation of *Macbeth*

Before starting this activity, the children need to be certain of the context for their adaptation of the story and will need to have considered how the storyboard will be constructed. You could offer them choices from the list below, constrain their choices, allocate each group to a particular approach or decide that all groups will follow the same method.

- ⊙ Enactment captured on digital camera. Key scenes are acted out in appropriate locations and digitally photographed.

- ⊙ Suitable locations for scenes downloaded from the internet. The children search the internet for photos of locations they feel are appropriate.

- ⊙ Scenes are enacted in the classroom and the characters are 'transferred' to locations found on the internet through the use of a photo-editing program.

- ⊙ Scenes are hand-drawn and scanned into the computer.

The organisation of this activity will be dependent on the approach(es) you decide to adopt. Whichever method is used, the scenes for the storyboard will have to be transferred to the master computer for each group at some point.

Activity 4: Completion of the presentation and rehearsal

Once the storyboard has been completed, the children need to work on the final slides which are designed to plead their case for funding for their movie. These could be completed collaboratively on the master computer but would be more effective if the group members assumed the roles designated by the webquest (director, costume designer, set designer/location manager, cameraman, etc.) and completed their slides individually for compilation into the master slide show (as in Activity 2).

Before making their presentation the children will need some rehearsal time. The easiest way to ensure involvement by all members of the group is to decide who will speak about each slide.

Activity 5: The presentations

Remind the children about the purpose of the activity and the evaluation criteria provided in the webquest. Distribute the evaluation sheets and explain their function.

In turn, the groups give their presentations to the rest of the class who complete the evaluation sheets. These are collected at the end of the activity to enable you to 'mark' the presentations.

Activity 6: The outcome and evaluation of the project

Having 'scored' the presentations using the information on the evaluation sheets, you present the decision of the shareholders to the class. Discuss the processes the children have gone through and ask them to speculate on how this compares with the processes which happen in the 'real' world of film making.

You could conclude the project by showing the children the website for a film currently in production. A useful starting point for finding this sort of information is the *Internet Movie Database* – www.imdb.com

What should the children know already?

What a presentation is and how a good presentation is structured

The skills needed for creating a presentation are not dissimilar to those needed to word process. A basic knowledge of how to enter text and some knowledge of formatting (e.g. emboldening, underlining, indenting) would enable the children to present their ideas more effectively.

Some background knowledge of Shakespeare and an outline of the story of *Macbeth*

As indicated in the description of the preliminary activity above, this could be achieved as part of ongoing literacy work, an introductory lesson, reading a class text (e.g. Leon Garfield's *Shakespeare Stories* (Puffin, 1997)), using a CD-ROM or showing them a video/DVD such as *The Animated Tales: Macbeth*.

What resources will I need?

Internet access and a computer suite and/or classroom computers

Webquests, as the name implies, require children to access information and ideas from the internet. The webquest format ensures that time is used effectively provided there are sufficient computers and access to the internet is reliable.

A webquest

An example webquest for this project is provided on the CD-ROM which accompanies this book. It is presented as a series of web pages. The folder containing the entire webquest website should be copied from the disc on to all the computers used by the children. It is important that the entire folder and its contents are transferred intact or the images and resources linked to the web pages will not function properly.

The webquest can be modified if you need to change some of the information or tasks to address the specific needs of your children. A web-authoring program such as *Microsoft FrontPage*, *WebEditor* (Namo), or *HotHTML 2001* (Web Software Systems) which can be downloaded free of charge from www.wsoftware.biz

A list of appropriate websites containing the information needed by the children

If you use the webquest on the CD-ROM, then the web links are included on the relevant page. These can be edited using a web-authoring program (see above) if you want to amend or add the links.

Alternatively, the web links could be provided as bookmarks in the web browser, or in a separate document (see 'What do I need to know?', below).

PowerPoint or a similar presentation program

Microsoft PowerPoint is the most well-known presentation program and the one which is most likely to be found on PCs as it is usually provided as part of *Microsoft Office*. If you do not have this installed on your computer, an alternative is *Impress* which is part of *Open Office*, available as a free download from www.openoffice.org

Educational presentation programs include:

⊙ *Textease Presenter* which is part of *Textease Studio* – see www. softease.com

⊙ *Slideshow* (BlackCat) – see www.blackcatsoftware.com

An example of a 'good' presentation

One example is provided on the CD-ROM that accompanies this book but, if you prefer alternatives, the internet will provide you with a wide range of examples. A good source for presentations, information and ideas appropriate for primary school is *PowerPoint in the Classroom*, available from http://www.actden.com/pp/

What do I need to know?

How to structure and manage a webquest

The pedagogy underpinning webquests has been well researched and documented. Refer to the *WebQuest* website (www.webquest.org) for more details. The premise underpinning webquests is that children need a clear context and focus to make more effective use of the information presented on the internet.

All webquests follow a similar pattern: Introduction – Task – Process – Evaluation. There are hundreds of webquests which can be viewed and used on the Webquest websites.

To familiarise yourself with webquests, read through the webquest for this project which is available on the CD-ROM accompanying the book.

How to create presentations using *PowerPoint* (or similar)

PowerPoint is one of the easiest *Microsoft Office* programs to use once you have understood its structure. Each screen in a *PowerPoint* presentation represents one of a number of slides which link together in sequence to form a slide show. Various tools and features can be used to design each slide but the essential components of a slide are text boxes and images. These can be positioned on each slide where needed. For added interest, the components on a slide can be animated – each line of text can be made to spiral onto the screen, for example – and transition effects can be added between slides.

The features of an effective presentation

As indicated above, *PowerPoint* includes a number of effects to enhance the appearance of a slide show. There is a tendency for inexperienced presenters to overdo the effects. As a general guide the following 'rules' could be used to ensure the children's slide shows are effective:

⊙ Bullet-point all the information on the slide
⊙ Use no more than six bullet points per slide
⊙ Use no more than six words per bullet point
⊙ Keep the same font throughout the slide show – so choose the most appropriate at the start
⊙ An image speaks a thousand words – so use images to sell your ideas
⊙ Never read what is on the screen to your audience – use it as a prompt

What will the children learn?

How to locate, identify and access information on the internet to address specific lines of enquiry

Although the webquest presents the children with hyperlinks to web pages already checked for content, the children will need to skim and scan or use page-searching tools to locate the specific information they need. Hence the focus is on extracting relevant information rather than searching for it.

How to structure information as part of a collaborative project

The allocation of roles within the groups helps to ensure the children will be finding specific information for their contribution to the presentation. This should help to ensure the slides are complementary. However, there might still be overlaps and occasionally some judicious editing may be needed. Whether this is done by the children working collaboratively, by an 'editor in chief' in each group or by the teacher is a decision you should make based on your knowledge of the children.

How to present information using ICT

Changing the focus of the information they find on the websites and the style in which it is presented for the intended audience is an important part of the project and should avoid the temptation to simply copy and paste chunks of text verbatim from the internet. You could include a practice task as a preliminary exercise or demonstrate the repurposing of a paragraph as part of your introduction to the project. This could be a useful shared writing task if you have an interactive whiteboard or data projection in your classroom.

Challenging the more able and supporting the less able: modifying the project for older and younger pupils

Adjusting the level of challenge in the webquest tasks

You could remove the links from the webquest to encourage the children to search for their own information – though this can prove time consuming and counter-productive. The webquest could be modified so that the stages the children go through is more heavily prescribed. This reduces the potential for learning outside the objectives for each session, but for those who are inexperienced or lacking in confidence (or collaborative skills), this might ensure the project runs more smoothly.

Adjusting the complexity of the presentation creation activities

You could provide the children with a ready-made template for their presentation. Each page could be pre-formatted so all the children have to do is insert the requisite information. Alternatively, you could structure the introductory activities with the presentation software even more carefully. This would lead to some uniformity in the presentations but would help to ensure that the right sort of information was provided. At the other extreme, those children who are very confident could work independently on their presentations.

Adjusting the level of support provided

Ensuring that each group includes at least one child who is a confident user of ICT could help to ensure that the groups work productively. However, the confident user could dominate the group and provide little opportunity for the others to contribute if the personality mix has not been carefully considered.

Anyone providing support (teacher, teaching assistant, helper or peer) needs to be briefed on the purpose of the activity and the most effective method of providing support.

Why teach this?

The data-gathering aspect of this project is less important than the thought which should be put into the preparation and design of the presentation. The children should recognise that the ICT presentation provides them with 'headlines' – a framework to guide and illustrate the live, spoken communication of their ideas.

If there is time, the children could make use of sound and/or digital video clips to reinforce their message. The technicalities of incorporating these media into *PowerPoint* are not immense, particularly if the children will be compiling their work on a laptop computer which will then be used for the presentation – minimising the complications of transferring large files from one computer to another.

QCA ICT Unit 5C: *Evaluating information, checking accuracy and questioning plausibility* and Unit 6D: *Using the internet to search large databases and to interpret information* are centred on gathering and interpreting information. These aspects are a subsidiary focus for this project which is designed to concentrate the children's attention more on the presentation of information and, more specifically, original ideas. However, this project complements most of the learning for both of these units and would act as a direct replacement for Unit 6A: *Multimedia presentation.*

The literacy focus for this project differs from that in Project 9 by placing emphasis on speaking and listening. The writing skills needed for developing the content of a multimedia presentation are quite different to those needed for a web page. The information on a slide should be succinct and abbreviated, conveying the essential details which can then be elaborated upon in the 'live' presentation. A web page has to be clear, unambiguous and free-standing.

Time could be spent outside the ICT activities developing the children's understanding of persuasive writing – how ideas need to be balanced with clear justification. For example, providing background information about previous filmic adaptations of *Macbeth* could help persuade the hypothetical audience that their decision to present the story as a power struggle between children in a school setting is worth their investment.

It is essential that the groups work closely together for this project. If they decide to enact their storyboards, the children will need to consider the visual impact of their pictures. Visual literacy and multimedia literacy are no less important in today's world than text-based literacy or 'letteracy' as defined by Seymour Papert (1993). The production of the presentation is the means to an end rather than an end in itself and so you need to consider carefully how much time you give the children to rehearse their presentations to ensure they are fully aware of the importance of conveying their information and ideas clearly and convincingly.

See also *Science* Project 7 (*Multimedia information source*) and *Humanities* Project 8 (*Making an information source*) for further ideas.

References and further reading

Garfield, L. (1997) *Shakespeare Stories*, illus. M. Foreman, Harmondsworth: Puffin.
Papert, S. (1993) *The Children's Machine: Rethinking School in the Age of the Computer*, New York: Basic Books.

Index